First-Rate Reading™:

Literature-Based Activities that Support Research-Based Instruction

Grade 1

by inda De Geronimo and

nne Diehl

Carson-Dellosa Publishing Company, Inc.
Greensboro, North Carolina

Credits
to First-Rate Reading™

Project Coordinator: Kelly Gunzenhauser

Editors: Ellen Holmes and Donna Walkush

Layout Design: Jon Nawrocik

Cover Design: Annette Hollister-Papp

Cover Illustration: Bill Neville

Illustrators: Bill Neville and Wayne Miller

Dedication
of First-Rate Reading™

To our families, especially our husbands Lee and Bob, for their continued support and encouragement, and to the excellent staff at Woodbrook School, Edison NJ for their suggestions. Also, special thanks to our first grade team: Kelly, Amanda, Carrie, Michele, Patty and Jodi.

ISBN 0-88724-250-2

Table of Contents
to *First-Rate Reading™*

• *What is Put Reading First?*
By now, most educators are familiar with the Put Reading First federal initiative. Part of the No Child Left Behind Act, Reading First is the culmination of research designed to identify best practices for reading teachers. Reading First holds teachers accountable for students' mastery of five very specific components of literacy: phonemic awareness, phonics, fluency, vocabulary, and comprehension. Practices that focus on these components are already in use by many teachers, and several states have received grants to implement Reading First programs.

• *How will the* First-Rate Reading *series help me teach reading?*
In addition to the fact that literacy is a basic and necessary skill, the love of books and the desire to share that love inspires many teachers. Even in the face of increased standardized testing and skill-based instruction, fine children's literature continues to be an important part of reading curriculums. This series helps teachers connect great literature with lessons that reinforce the components of Reading First by:
  • providing additional phonemic awareness and phonics practice for students who need it
  • reinforcing phonics concepts with activities that conform to an existing, sequential phonics program
  • making teaching vocabulary strategies fun and relevant
  • creating opportunities for students to practice fluency skills with age-appropriate texts
  • engaging students in discussions and activities that help them comprehend what they read and apply those meanings to other literature and to their own lives

• *Why were these children's books chosen for this series?*
Teaching reading is much easier when students (and teachers) have a desire to read. These books were chosen because students respond to real, excellent literature (many are Caldecott Medal and Newbery Medal winners), and because they are student and teacher favorites. Attention is paid to old favorites, such as *Green Eggs and Ham* and *Frog and Toad Together*, as well as modern classics like *If You Take a Mouse to School* and *Because of Winn-Dixie*. There is truly something for every reader to enjoy.

• *Some activities and reproducibles seem very advanced/very easy for my class. How do I adjust them to fit different levels?*
After completing beginning-of-the-year assessments, you should have an idea of students' reading and writing skills. What may take longer to assess is their different abilities to work independently. At the first grade level, you should direct the activities by doing them in whole-class, small-group, or partner settings. Additionally, make the reproducibles more accessible by modeling what students should do, reading all words and directions aloud to them, saying the names of pictures and the sounds of letters, etc. For activities which require students to write, consider having students dictate their answers, since many young children cannot write more than a few short words. Also, consider having students color every page on which there is art, both to give them fine-motor-skill practice and to let them make even dictated work "their own."

• *How do I actually use the children's books with the activities?*
Some activities use the actual text from the books, while others use themes that are similar to those in the books. For example, a phonics activity based around *Click, Clack, Moo: Cows That Type* looks at the ick and ack word families, with *Click, Clack* as the examples. Other activities for *Click, Clack, Moo: Cows That Type* use the farm animal references for alphabet work, and the text for lessons about fantasy and fiction. Page numbers in each children's book are referenced, but bear in mind that some books do not have page numbers, and that numbering may change according to which edition you use.

• *How do I match these activities to the phonics system I have to follow, and how do I know when to choose which lesson?*
In the Table of Contents, all of the activities are listed by type. Some of the activities are general in what they teach (making predictions, alphabet practice, etc.) but are unique in how they are executed. Other activities are very specific in what they teach (/g/ sounds, ot word family, etc.). Since most beginning reading programs are driven by the order in which phonemic awareness and phonics elements are taught, it may be most convenient to refer to the Phonemic Awareness and Phonics key below, and base literature choices on how your program's phonics lessons correspond to the phonics key below.

Phonemic Awareness/Phonics
Key Page References

long /a/–128
/ar/ sound–30
c (hard and soft)–28, 110
short /e/–18, 20
long /e/ (e, ee, ea)–38, 150
/h/–58
short /i/–40, 50, 88, 98
long /i/–40, 88, 98
/l/–88
l-controlled vowels–68
/oo/–38, 68
ou–30, 70
ow–30, 70
r-controlled vowels–8, 30, 130
/s/–68

alphabet–30, 138, 140
animal sounds–8
blending sounds–58
consonant blends–60, 90, 100, 108, 118, 120, 130
consonant digraphs–50, 70, 120
ending phonemes–58
initial letters–90, 140
initial phonemes–48, 58, 68, 138
letter names and sounds–138
missing vowels–70
print awareness–80
rhymes (words, word families, phonemes)–8, 10, 20, 28, 40, 48, 50, 60, 78, 80, 88, 90, 100, 128, 130, 148
sound spelling–80
sounding out words–20
speed spelling–80
syllable work–20, 28, 50, 118, 120, 128, 150
vowels–100, 110
word endings–108

Pronunciation Guide
to *First-Rate Reading*™

This book uses very simple descriptions of sounds in order to make the activities easily adaptable to your school's phonics program. These guidelines are not meant to be a full phonics program. In **every** case, use the phoneme and phonics cues that your phonics program recommends. See the chart below for specific information about the sounds presented in this series.

Vowel Sounds
These symbols encompass the sounds made by each combination of vowels and consonants. The letter combinations are paired with example words that make the sounds.

short /a/ and long /a/
- long /a/ includes ai as in rain, a_e as in cake, and ea as in break

short /e/ and long /e/
- short /e/ includes ea as in breath
- long /e/ includes ea as in steal, ee as in steel, ei as in either, ie as in thief, and y as in happy

short /i/ and long /i/
- short /i/ includes y as in myth (Note: some phonics programs deem ing as short /i/)
- long /i/ includes ie as in tried, i_e as in ice, igh as in high, ight as in night, and y as in my

short /o/ and long /o/
- long /o/ includes oa as in goat, o_e as in role, ou as in soul, and ow as in slow

short /u/ and long /u/
- short /u/ includes oo as in blood
- long /u/ may include ew as in few, ou as in youth, ue as in blue, oo as in scoot (Different phonics programs consider either /yu/ and/or /oo/ as long /u/)

Vowel Combinations, Vowel Teams, and Vowel-Consonant Teams
Difficult vowel combinations are treated individually. Each is paired with an example word that makes the sound.
- /au/ as in caught
- /aw/ as in saw (/au/ and /aw/ may differ depending on regional dialect
- /oi/ and /oy/ as in poise and joy
- /oo/ as in spoon, foot, or short /u/ as in blood
- /ou/ and /ow/ as in loud and cow

R-Controlled Vowels and Diphthongs
Rather than substitute the *schwa* character (ə) for r-controlled vowels and diphthongs, they are listed with example words. This helps remind teachers to differentiate, for example, between the /or/ sound in the word *for* and the /or/ sound in the word *doctor*, so that students don't over-pronounce the *or* as *doctor* or the *or* in *for* as *fur*. Additionally, many students who are learning to read find the schwa confusing in print and will learn the correct local pronunciation without additional coaching.

Consonant Sounds
/b/	/d/	/f/	/g/ (hard g as in goat)	/h/
/j/ (soft g as in gem)	/k/ (hard c as in cat)	/l/	/m/	/n/
/p/	/kw/ (for q with u)	/r/	/s/ (soft c as in cell)	/t/
/v/	/w/	/ks/ (x as in fox)	/y/	/z/

Digraphs
/ch/	/sh/ (ss as in mission, ch as in machine)	/th/ as in this (not voiced)
/th/ as in then (voiced)	/wh/ as in whale	/zh/ as in vision

Are You My Mother?

by P. D. Eastman
(Random House, 1960)

Are You My Mother? is a delightful story about a baby bird who hatches from his egg and does not see his mother. The baby bird decides to find her, jumps out of his nest, and interviews several possible mommy "candidates." This book can be used to teach verb tense; /ir/, /ur/, and /er/ sounds; role-playing, innovations; and science (classification of living and nonliving objects).

Related books: *Is Your Mama a Llama?* by Deborah Guarino (Scholastic, 1991); *Mama, Do You Love Me?* by Barbara M. Joosse (Chronicle Books, 1998)

Phonemic Awareness Activities
for *Are You My Mother?*

Pre-reading Activity: Teach the r-controlled vowel sound (or vowel variant schwa /ur/) sound. Write *bird* and *mother* on the board and read them aloud. Underline the ir and er. Ask students what sound they both make. Distribute the Mother and Baby Birds reproducible (page 9). Have each student cut out the baby birds and the nest, and place the baby birds in a pile. Read a list of words. Each time a student hears the /ur/ sound he should place a baby bird in the nest. After you read the list, have students count the baby birds in their nests to see how well they listened. Continue the game with other lists. List suggestions are (1) *dirt, bear, join, shirt, fern, boy, jump, Fred, stern, hat, chair, red*; (2) *term, team, pot, table, germ, stir, book, hand, fry, soap, pen, sir*; (3) *bird, talk, drink, birth, third, her, pink, mother, dancer, clerk, herb, skirt*; and (4) *nerve, white, basket, nest, swerve, squirt, cat, dog, herd, verb, smirk, thirst*.

During-reading Activity: Explain that *Are You My Mother?* is about a baby bird who meets many things while searching for his mother. Each time the bird meets someone or something, let a volunteer tell the class what sound that animal or thing would make. After students are familiar with the sound of each animal or item, read the story again. Pause after the baby bird asks his question so that students can say the sound of that animal or thing. Sounds that students might suggest are meow, cluck, woof, moo, beep, chug, zoom, and snort. For each sound have the students name a rhyming word.

Post-reading Activity: Write the word *fur* on the board. Ask students what sounds they hear in the word. Explain that the letters ur also make the /ur/ sound like ir and er in *bird* and *her*. Play the baby bird game again (from the pre-reading activity), this time adding ur words to the lists such as *urge, curl, burn, turn, churn, lurk, nurse, purse, hurt, blurt,* and *spurt*.

Name_____ Date _____

Cut out the nest and each baby bird. Put a baby bird on the nest each time you hear your teacher read an /ur/ sound like in *bird* and *mother.*

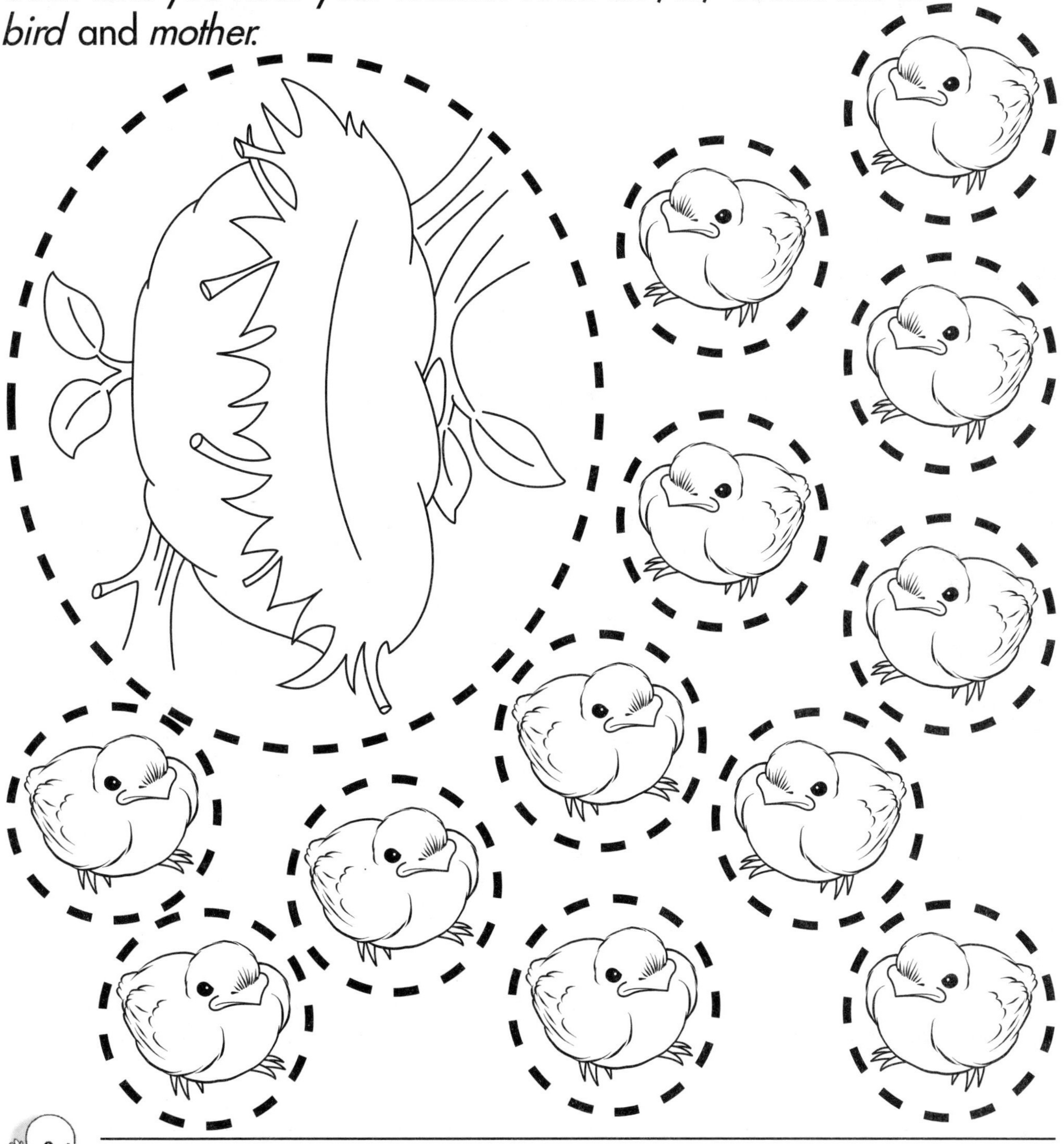

Phonics Activities

for *Are You My Mother?*

Pre-reading Activity: Students will hear the word *not* many times in this story. Prior to this activity, draw a large cooking pot on a piece of chart paper. Write the word *not* on the board. Ask a volunteer to read the word. Erase the letter n and ask students to repeat the sound that the remaining letters make when blended together. Write the letter p at the beginning of the word and say "pot." Inform students that they can make other words by continuing to replace just the first letter. Explain that the words they can form in this manner are part of a *word family*. Have students work in pairs or small groups to create new words containing the /ot/ ending. When students are finished, ask for volunteers to give you the new words they formed. Write their new words on the drawing of the pot. Accept nonsense words, but discuss which words are real and which are not at a later time. You may want to underline or circle the real words.

During-reading Activity: Review the ot words from the pre-reading activity. Explain that students will hear one of these words repeated often in the story (*not*). As you read the story aloud, have students clap their hands every time they hear this ot word. When they clap their hands, pause and ask a volunteer to say another word from the ot word family. Continue until you finish the book, or until students run out of words from the ot family.

Post-reading Activity: Give a large piece of construction paper and a copy of the OT Word Family reproducible (page 11) to each student. Explain to students that they will cut out the word cards on the reproducibles and then use them to make sentences. Allow students to use more than one ot word in each sentence. Tell students that the words with uppercase letters should be used at the beginnings of sentences. Depending on students' levels, you may choose to have students work with partners or in groups. Once they have sentences that make sense, have them put the sentences aside and try to make other sentences. When students have made as many sentences as possible, have them paste their sentences on the construction paper. Remind them to put periods at the ends of their sentences. Challenge students to try to use as many of the ot cards as they can. Have students share their sentences with the class when they are finished and point out the ot words as they share.

Name_____ Date _____

Cut out each word card. Use the word cards to make sentences. Put a period at the end of each sentence. Use as many cards as you can.

not	pot	cot	dot	lot
got	tot	The	The	This
A	A	is	is	is
has	has	a	a	red
big	boy	girl	.	. . .

Vocabulary Activities
for *Are You My Mother?*

Pre-reading Activity: Write the following words on a piece of chart paper: *where, home, know, right, kitten, happened, mother, bird, jumped, looked, away, went, down, could, walk, boat, plane.* Tell students that they will see these words in *Are You My Mother?* Ask volunteers to read the words and define them. When a student defines a word correctly, tell him that he will become the expert for that word, and have him write the word on an index card. Put the student's name on the back of the card and keep it for use in the next two activities. Continue until all of the words are defined correctly. You may want to give clues to help each student receive a card.

During-reading Activity: Have students read the words on their index cards from the pre-reading activity (above) to the class. Next, give a sentence strip to each student. Ask students to look up their words in dictionaries and write the definitions on sentence strips. (Help students write if they need it.) Then, have them stand up and read their cards and definitions to their classmates. Read the book aloud. Tell students to listen for their words and turn their cards facedown when they hear their words read. Some students will hear their words more than once. Check to see that all students have their cards facedown when you have finished reading. If there are several students that didn't hear their words, read the story again. As you read, occasionally stop and review the sentences in which the words were found. Collect all cards and sentence strips for use in the next activity.

Post-reading Activity: Prior to this activity, draw a tree trunk on a piece of bulletin board paper and attach it to a bulletin board. (You may also use an existing bulletin board set for this activity.) Return students' index cards and sentence strips from the pre-reading and during-reading activities. Have each student read her word and definition to the class. Next, ask each student to write a new sentence using her vocabulary word on a piece of paper. Check each student's sentence and have her carefully copy it on a piece of brown sentence strip. Hand out copies of the Nests of Knowledge reproducible (page 13). Have each student copy her word on the card that the bird is holding. Then, let her color and cut out the bird and nest, and tape the bird to the nest and the nest to both sentence strips. As students finish, attach the sentence strips to the tree trunk as branches. Title the bulletin board "Nests of Knowledge."

Nests of Knowledge

vocabulary reproducible for
Are You My Mother?

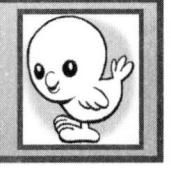

Name______________________________ Date ______________

Write your vocabulary word on the card that the baby bird is holding. Color and cut out the bird and the nest. Tape the bird to the nest. Then, tape the bird and nest to the sentence you wrote using the word.

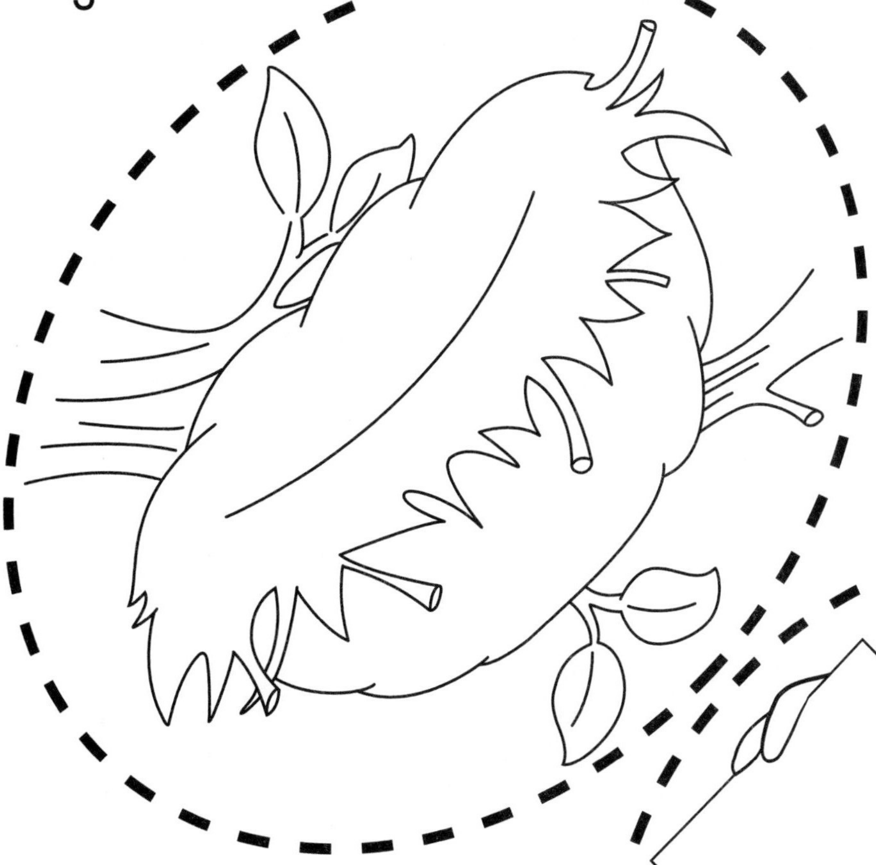

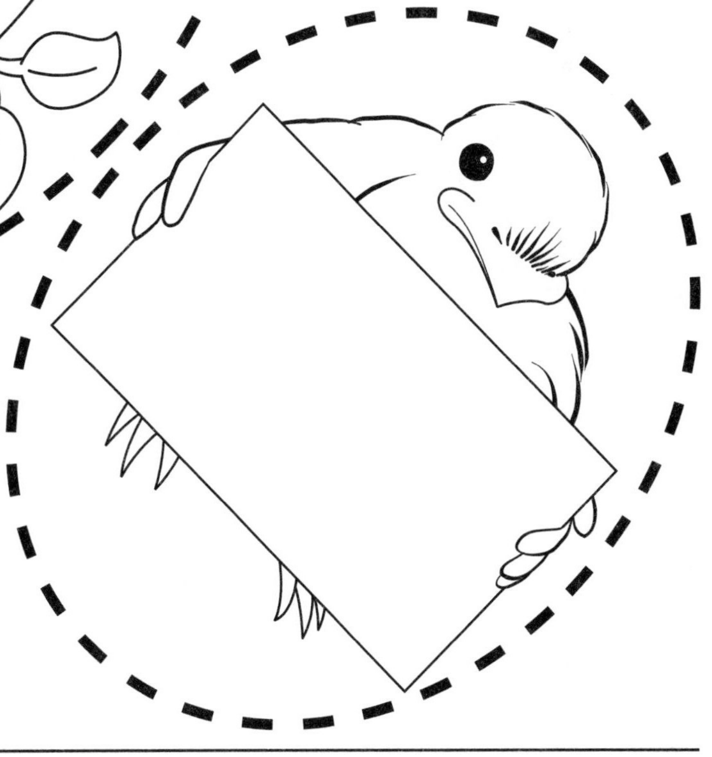

Fluency Activities

for *Are You My Mother?*

Pre-reading Activity: Tell students that the baby bird in this story is happiest when he is home in his nest with his mother. Lead a discussion about how nice it is to be home after a hard day at work or school. Distribute the Home Sweet Home reproducible (page 15). Read the poem to students. Tell them that reading poetry fluently makes a poem more fun to listen to, like reading a story fluently makes a story more fun to hear. Assign half of the class the first line in each stanza and the rest of the class the second line in each stanza. Give students time to practice silently. Help students with some words, if necessary. After enough time has passed, bring students back together and have the members of each group read their parts of the poem together. Challenge students to add lines to the poem showing reasons why they like to be at home. Share additions with the class. To extend the activity, have students write their additions to the poem on the backs of their papers, then illustrate their favorite aspects of their homes.

During-reading Activity: Explain to students that there is a narrator in *Are You My Mother?* who will tell parts of the story, but there are places where the baby bird and other animals will speak. Tell students that you are going to read the story to them and they should listen for characters' exact words. Read the story aloud to students. Ask them if they can explain when characters are speaking in the story. How do they know? Draw quotation marks on the board and explain that quotation marks are used to show the exact words a character says. Ask a volunteer to describe how each animal might sound. (The baby bird might have a squeaky voice, the cow a deep voice, the dog a tired voice, etc.) Ask volunteers to read specific parts with these expressions. Read the story a second time with students reading their assigned parts.

Post-reading Activity: Review with students that this story has a narrator telling the story and exact quotes from the characters. Explain that they are going to put on a play. (Students will not memorize parts; they will just read lines from the book.) Since there will not be enough characters for all students, either have more than one student read a part or have them perform the play more than once. You may also assign the narrator's role as a chorally-read part. Next, have students make costumes for their characters. Keep them simple, such as a kerchief for the mother bird, a beak for the baby bird, ears and a tail for the kitten, feathers for the hen, long ears or a collar for the dog, horns or a bell for the cow, paper wings for the plane, wheels for the car, a mast for the boat, and a dowel or stick with a scoop for the steam shovel. Provide construction paper, crayons, and rubber bands or string to make costumes. After costumes are made, have each student come on "stage" when it is his turn to read his part. Remind students to read with expression and fluency. As students get comfortable with the play, allow them to add motions. Invite parents or other classes to see the performance.

Name _____   Date _____

Read the poem and follow your teacher's instructions. On the right side of the page, draw a picture of your favorite thing about home or illustrate parts of the poem.

Home

Home is the place to be,
It's where I find my family.

Home is the place to be,
When I fall and skin my knee.

Home is the place to be,
When my tummy troubles me.

Home is the place to be,
When my family plays with me.

Home is the place to be,
When my bed is warm for me.

Home is the place to be,
When my puppy jumps on me.

There's nowhere else I want to be,
How 'bout you? Do you agree?

Comprehension Activities
for *Are You My Mother?*

Pre-reading Activity: Have students sit in a circle or on a rug. Ask students to tell you about the things their parents (or guardians) do for them. Write their answers on a piece of chart paper. When students have finished, review the list with them. Show students the cover of the book and read the title. Explain that they are going to read a story about a baby bird that is looking for his mother. Ask students why it is important for the baby bird to find his mother. Ask, "What does a mother bird do for her babies? Where do you think the baby bird will go to find his mother?"

During-reading Activity: Prior to this activity, create a chart with two columns. Label one column *Living* and the other column *Nonliving.* Display the chart so that students can see it. Ask students if they know the difference between living and nonliving things, and how they can tell if something is alive. (It needs nourishment, shelter, light, etc.) Explain that the baby bird will ask everybody and everything it sees if they are his mother. Students' job is to classify each object as either living or nonliving. Read the story to students. As the baby bird asks, "Are you my mother?" pause so that students can tell you in which category to put the animal or object. Review the list when you are finished. Ask students what response the baby bird received from each animal or thing. Ask, "Why didn't the bird get a response from the car? The boat? The plane? Did the steam shovel answer the baby bird?" Then, direct students to fold handwriting paper in half lengthwise to create columns and label one column *Living* and the other *Nonliving.* Have students copy the words from the chart and challenge them to add things to both sides of their papers. Have students share lists with classmates and allow them to add additional living and nonliving things to their own lists as they hear things they did not think of.

Post-reading Activity: Tell students that they are going to change and add to the story before the baby bird gets put back into his nest. This is called an *innovation.* Explain that they will decide who or what the baby bird meets next on his journey. Of course, the baby bird will ask, "Are you my mother?" Tell students that they must also find different ways for the baby bird to get back into his nest. Distribute the Innovation reproducible (page 17) to students. Have them work independently on this page. When students are finished, have them read innovations aloud and decide if each new animal or thing the baby bird meets is living or nonliving. Add each new character to the chart from the during-reading activity.

Name_____   Date _____

Continue the story of the baby bird's search for his mother. Who or what do you think the baby bird will meet next? Fill in the blanks. Use the last part to make up a new ending and describe how the baby bird gets home.

So, the baby bird went on until he came to a _____.
"Are you my mother?" he asked the _____.
The_____said "_____
_____."

Next, the baby bird went on until he came to a _____.
"Are you my mother?" he asked the _____.
The_____said "_____
_____."

Finally, the baby bird saw a_____.
"Are you my mother?" he asked the _____.

The _____

_____

_____

_____

_____.

The End

Chickens Aren't the Only Ones
by Ruth Heller

(Grosset & Dunlap, 1981)

This wonderful book about eggs that chickens and other animals lay is illustrated with detailed, colorful pictures to accompany the rhythmic text. It includes information about wild birds, reptiles, dinosaurs, amphibians, fish, spiders, insects, and even two egg-laying mammals. The life cycle of the butterfly is also addressed. Use this book to teach a variety of science-related activities as well as the use of rhyming to tell a story.

Related books: *Animals and Their Eggs* by Renne (Gareth Stevens, August 2000); *An Egg Is an Egg* by Nicki Weiss (Paperstar, 1996); *How to Hide a Butterfly* by Ruth Heller (Price Stern Sloan Pub., 1992)

Phonemic Awareness Activities
for *Chickens Aren't the Only Ones*

Pre-reading Activity: Make students "eggsperts" at finding the short /e/ sound. Copy the "Eggspert" Eggs reproducible (page 19) on card stock. Have each student cut out an egg and tape a craft stick to the back of it for a handle. Review the sound of short /e/ as in *hen, pen,* and *send.* Ask students for other words with the short /e/ sound. Next, ask if the word *chicken* has a short /e/ sound. Explain to students that many words have the short /e/ sound, but they have to be really good listeners to hear it. Tell students that when they hold these special short /e/ eggs, they will become experts at finding short /e/ words. Next, read the following words aloud: *chickens, lay, boil, aren't, every, fry, leave, extinct, reptiles, legs, only, when, bird, ostrich, hummingbird, protected, then, tadpoles, shed, them, amphibians, everyone, tell,* and *fish.* Have students hold up the short /e/ eggs when they hear a word with a short /e/ sound. After the activity, discuss any short /e/ words they missed.

During-reading Activity: Have students use their short /e/ eggs for this activity. Tell students that the words from the pre-reading activity are words they will hear in the story. Read *Chickens Aren't the Only Ones* aloud. Each time students hear a word with the short /e/ sound, they should hold up their eggs. Reward students with jelly or marshmallow "eggs," or other egg-shaped treats.

Post-reading Activity: Go on a short /e/ egg hunt. Use plastic eggs or the short /e/ eggs from the pre-reading activity. Assign students to two teams. Have one team cover their eyes. Tell students on the other team that they have one minute to find things in the room with the short /e/ sound. When they find something, they should hide an egg next to it. When time is up, let students from the first team find the eggs, say the sound of short /e/, and then say names of the items. Let teams switch roles and continue until students run out of short /e/ items.

"Eggspert" Eggs
phonemic awareness reproducible for
Chickens Aren't the Only Ones

Name_____ Date _____

Cut out the egg on this page. Glue or tape a craft stick to the back to make a handle. Your teacher will tell you what to do next.

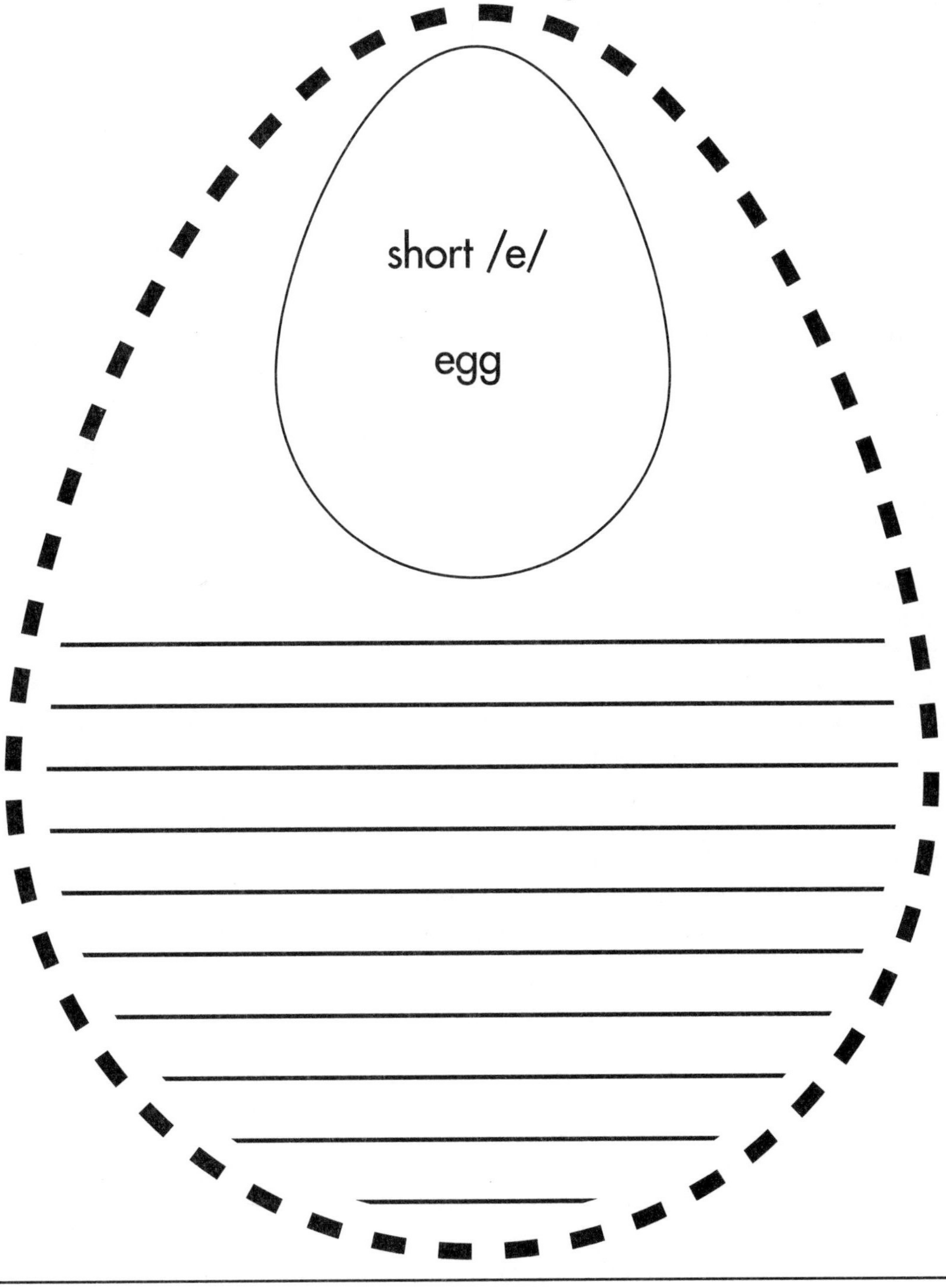

short /e/

egg

Phonics Activities

for *Chickens Aren't the Only Ones*

Pre-reading Activity: Provide students with copies of the "Eggspert" Eggs reproducible (page 19). Review the sound of short /e/ with students. Preview the book cover and pictures and have students predict some of the short /e/ words from the story. Have them write the words on the lines provided. Help students spell harder words. If students have trouble filling in all of the lines, tell them they can use any short /e/ words they can think of. Have students share their words with the class, and instruct them to watch or listen for the words they wrote on their eggs as you read the story.

During-reading Activity: *Chickens Aren't the Only Ones* contains many words that will be difficult for students to read. Explain to students that bigger words are easier to read if they sound them out one syllable at a time. Read the story aloud. Stop and have students count the syllables in some of the big words, such as *hummingbird, crocodile, dinosaur, salamander, amphibian, octopus, caterpillar, anteater, platypus,* and *oviparous,* by clapping the syllables. Write the words you clap on the board or a piece of chart paper. After reading, show students the words you have written and draw lines where you would divide the syllables. Practice sounding out each word syllable by syllable. Distribute the We Clap for Big Words reproducible (page 21). Have students cut out the puzzle pieces and put the syllables together to form words. Let students keep these pieces for practice at another time or have them paste their finished puzzles onto construction paper.

Post-reading Activity: Prior to this activity, cut out egg shapes and punch a hole at the top of each egg. Place the eggs in a pile at the front of the classroom. Have students work in pairs for this activity. Write the words *pair* and *share* on the board. Ask students what they can tell you about those words. (They rhyme.) Tell students that they are going to work in pairs and they are going to share work. Review rhyming words with students and tell them that the rhyming words in *Chickens Aren't the Only Ones* are not easy to find. Explain that students will go on "egg hunts." Each time they find a pair of rhyming words, have students come to the front of the classroom and take two blank eggs from the pile. After students have found all of the rhyming words, have them work together to use their rhyming words to make matching eggs. Each pair should write each rhyming word on an egg, and then color each set of rhyming eggs exactly the same to show the pair rhymes. Finally, have students string their eggs and hang them either on a bulletin board or from the ceiling. Title the display "Eggsactly Alike." When it is time to take down the display, place the rhyming eggs in a center for students to review.

We Clap for Big Words
phonics reproducible for
Chickens Aren't the Only Ones

Name_____ Date _____

Cut out each puzzle piece. Each piece has one part of a word (a syllable) on it. Fit the pieces together to make words from the book.

bird

er

ant

oc

din

saur

o

ming

o

to

plat

y

dile

croc

eat

pus

hum

pus

Vocabulary Activities
for *Chickens Aren't the Only Ones*

Pre-reading Activity: Use this book to give students an opportunity to learn animal classification. Prior to this activity, create a chart with the following categories on it: *birds, reptiles, amphibians, fish, insects,* and *mammals.* (Add *mollusks* if you think students will be able to identify animals in this category.) List an example for each category and title the chart "Oviparous Animals." Show students the cover of the book and read the title aloud. Ask students what they think the title might mean. After discussion, tell students that animals other than chickens lay eggs and they will learn about many of them in this book. Show them the chart. Explain that *oviparous* means laying eggs. Ask students to predict animals that lay eggs. Write all suggestions on the chart in pencil. After reading the book, make corrections, changes, or additions to the chart in marker.

During-reading Activity: Read *Chickens Aren't the Only Ones* aloud. Check the animal chart from the pre-reading activity to see how many of the students' predictions were correct. Reread the story and show the illustrations again to help students remember all of the animals. Add new animals to the chart. Hand out the Oviparous Animal Categories reproducible (page 23). Have students color the animals. Then, have them work in groups to draw lines to match animals that are in the same categories. Students may also work independently and use the book to complete this activity. Then, help students label the reproducible with animal and/or category names from the book. When students are finished, ask volunteers to read each category and its corresponding animal names.

Post-reading Activity: Using one copy of the Oviparous Animal Categories reproducible (page 23) from the during-reading activity, cut out the animals. Place the animal pictures in a hat or basket. Create a set of index cards with the categories on them and place them on a table or desk, or at a center. Have each student choose a picture from the container and give clues to help his classmates guess that animal. After they have guessed, have the student say the name of his picture and place it under the correct category on the table. Continue until all of the pictures have been used. For review, call out the name of an animal and have the class call out the category, or call out the category and have a student say an animal name that belongs in the category.

Oviparous Animal Categories
vocabulary reproducible for
Chickens Aren't the Only Ones

Name_____ Date _____

Color the pictures. Read *Chickens Aren't the Only Ones* to find the category for each animal. Draw lines to connect each set of animals that are from the same category.

Fluency Activities

for *Chickens Aren't the Only Ones*

Pre-reading Activity: Read the Hatching Eggs poem (page 25) aloud. Discuss what students "see" as you read the poem. Have each student cut out a copy of the poem and glue it to a large sheet of paper. Then, have her draw a picture of a child watching eggs hatch. Allow pairs to practice reading the poem together. When students are ready, read the poem chorally. After they have read, display the pictures.

During-reading Activity: The words in this book are slightly harder than usual since they give specific names of animals. Students will need extra time to practice these words before they can read the story fluently. Begin by reading the story aloud to the class. Read it a second time and have students read the capitalized animal names together for extra practice. Next, have small groups practice reading the different animal categories in the book. One group can read the beginning, another group can read about birds, and so on. Then, have each group read its section of the book to the class.

Post-reading Activity: Tell students that when they sing, they are usually fluent because the music keeps going, so they do, too! Using the list of animals created in the vocabulary pre-reading activity, challenge the class to replace the words of a familiar song with the names of these animals. Allow students to choose a song they know, then complete this activity as a class. Accept all answers. Explain that the song does not have to rhyme. For example, using the tune from "Row, Row, Row, Your Boat," students could sing the following song:

Bird, snail, frog and fish,
Mothers all lay eggs.
Patiently, patiently, patiently wait—
Hatching them takes days.

Toad, snake, crocodile,
Mothers all lay eggs.
Patiently, patiently, patiently wait—
Hatching them takes days.

Hatching Eggs

fluency reproducible for
Chickens Aren't the Only Ones

Name_____   Date _____

Read the poem. Color the picture. Cut along the line. Glue the poem to a large sheet of paper. Then, draw a picture of a child watching the eggs hatch.

- -

Hatching

I found an egg when I was two,
It was small and round and blue.

I saw the nest from where it came,
There were four more that looked the same.

The mother bird sat on the eggs,
I saw her head but not her legs.

The father bird just stood nearby,
I know he was a really proud guy.

The eggs hatched, and I watched the birds grow.
Wow, they put on a terrific show!

Now I know just what birds do,
When they have eggs that are small and blue.

by Robert C. Diehl

Comprehension Activities
for *Chickens Aren't the Only Ones*

Pre-reading Activity: Show students the cover of *Chickens Aren't the Only Ones*. Ask them to name the animal on the front cover (hen or chicken). Ask students what they know about chickens. Write their responses on the board or a piece of chart paper. Then, direct their attention to the title of the book and read it aloud. Ask students to predict what the title means. Refer back to the chart and ask students to pick what they think other animals do that chickens do, too. Star their answers and tell them that they will look at them again after you have read the story.

During-reading Activity: Tell students that they are going to choose animals (as you read the book) to complete an activity later. Pause while reading to discuss the many types of animals that lay eggs, as well as the differences among the groups. Pause for each student to write down the name of one animal from the book. Distribute the Animal Clues reproducible (page 27). Then, explain that students should create clues to help classmates guess the animals they chose. Instruct each student to write a clue about her animal on the cracked egg shells so that part of the clue is on each half. On the blank egg, she should draw and color the animal she chose. Help each student use a paper fastener to attach the whole egg behind the two cracked shells. Students should be able to read the clue on each shell half and then open the shell to reveal the animal inside. Allow students to read their clues to the class and select volunteers to guess the answers. Place the eggs in a center for students to practice solving.

Post-reading Activity: Before beginning this activity, write the following story starters on a piece of chart paper: *A bird fell on my head. A baby platypus stole my pie! I found a duck in my Easter basket! A mother snake made a nest in my bed! A crocodile laid her eggs in my sandbox! I found turtle eggs on the beach! There's an egg sac hanging outside of my window!* Ask students if they were surprised to find out that so many animals lay eggs. Show them the story starters and read each one aloud. Ask each student to choose one story starter, or make up one of his own, and write a story. Allow students to illustrate their stories, if desired. When stories are completed, have students share them with the class. As each student reads his story, discuss what the students learned about that animal from reading *Chickens Aren't the Only Ones*.

Animal Clues
comprehension reproducible for
Chickens Aren't the Only Ones

Name_____ Date _____

Choose one of the animals from the book. Write a clue about that animal on the pieces of cracked shell. Draw a picture of your animal on the egg without a crack. Cut out the egg and the cracked shell. Use a paper fastener to put the shell and the egg together.

CLICK, CLACK, MOO
Cows That Type

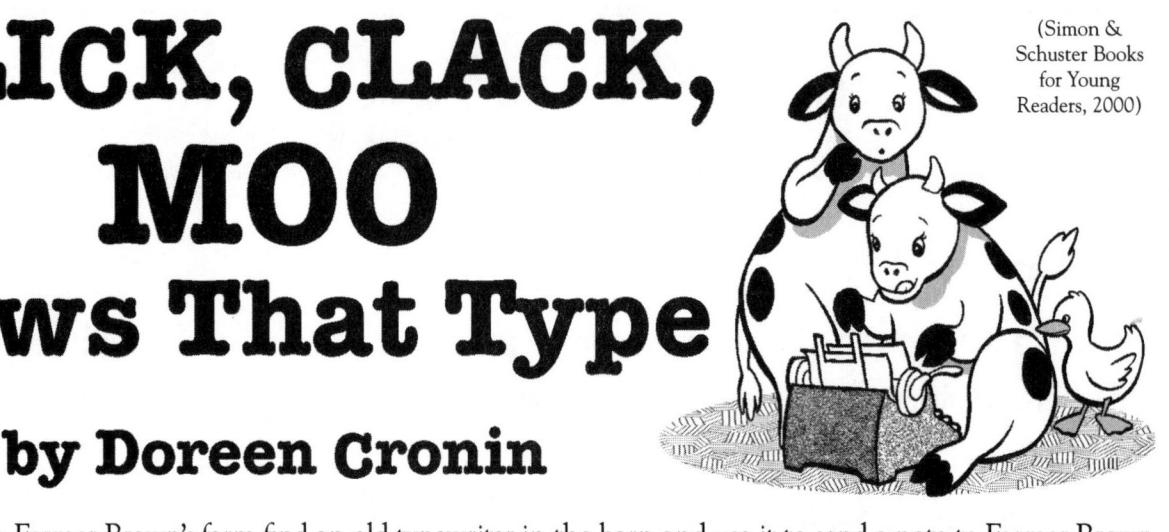

(Simon & Schuster Books for Young Readers, 2000)

by Doreen Cronin

The cows on Farmer Brown's farm find an old typewriter in the barn and use it to send a note to Farmer Brown asking for electric blankets. When Farmer Brown refuses their request, the cows go on strike. Duck, considered a neutral party, delivers another note to Farmer Brown suggesting a compromise. Farmer Brown agrees to the compromise only to find another note—the ducks are asking for a diving board! Students can have fun writing notes and using onomatopoeia as they read this clever story.

Related books: *The Cow That Went OINK* by Bernard Most (Red Wagon, 1990); *When Cows Come Home* by David L. Harrison (Boyds Mills Press, 2001)

Phonemic Awareness Activities
for *Click, Clack, Moo: Cows That Type*

Pre-reading Activity: Have students identify the initial sound in the word *cows*. Let them search the room for other things that begin with the /k/ sound. Say *cows* with other words they suggest to see if they can hear the /k/ sound in each. Play a riddle game with students. Give examples such as, "I am thinking of another word for *glass*. It is something you can drink from. What is it? (cup)." Give examples for the words *cake* and *cap*. Say all three words. Ask students to repeat the sound they hear at the beginning of each word. Then, ask them to think of riddles about words that begin with the /k/ sound to share with the class.

During-reading Activity: Many words in the story are difficult to say. Repeat the following words for students as you read: *impossible, impatient, problem, electric, blankets, typewriter, furious, neutral, party, ultimatum, emergency, meeting, exchange*. As you say each word, have students pretend to "type" on their desks by tapping with fingers for each syllable. Write the words in columns on the board according to the number of syllables they have. (Refer to the vocabulary section for ideas on how to teach these words meanings.)

Post-reading Activity: In the book title, there are two words that have only one different letter. Ask students to identify the two words (*click* and *clack*). Ask them to take off the cl in each word and say the endings of these words. Play a hot-potato game with word endings. Have students sit in a circle. Give two students the cutouts from the Ick and Ack reproducible (page 29). Play a recording of "The Farmer in the Dell" as students pass the cutouts. When the music stops, have each student who is holding a cutout stand and call out a new word that ends with the sound. Play until each student has had a turn to participate or until all possible words are exhausted. Students can use blends and digraphs as well as individual consonant sounds to create words.

Name_____ Date _____

Use the two typewriter cutouts to help students play the game described in the post-reading phonemic awareness section.

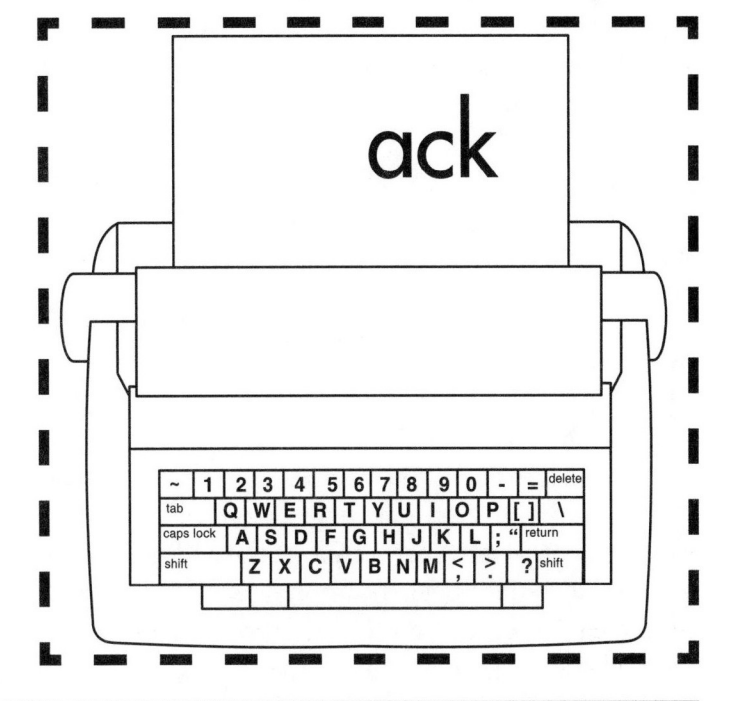

Phonics Activities
for *Click, Clack, Moo: Cows That Type*

Pre-reading Activity: Explain to students that some combinations of vowels stand for different sounds. For example, ow in *cow* and ou in *out* both make the same sound. Provide several copies of the book and have students work in pairs to find words in the book containing the ow or ou spelling pattern. They should be able to find *growing, ground, own, how, found, couldn't, enough, now, cows, brown, around,* and *outside.* Have them compare their lists of words, then collect the lists. Write the words on the board. Explain that *growing, own, couldn't,* and *enough* do not fit with the rest of the words that have the same sound as in *cow* or *out.* Ask students to suggest other ow or ou words with the same sound as in *growing.* List the words that they suggest in a separate column. Give each student two Flowers Say Ow! reproducibles (page 31). In the centers, have each student write *ou/ow.* Challenge students to search for words that contain ou/ow and have the same sound as in *cow* or *out,* and other words that have ou/ow and have the same sound as in *grow.* Have them write the words that rhyme with *flower* on one flower's petals, and the words that rhyme with *grow* on the other flower's petals. Title a bulletin board "How Does Our Garden Grow?" After students lightly color their petals, staple the flowers to the board to create a garden. To complete this activity with words from the ar word family, place a large barn on the bulletin board and repeat with another set of patterns. (See during-reading activity.)

During-reading Activity: Discuss that the setting of the story is a farm and that one of the main characters is Farmer Brown. Write the words *farm* and *farmer* on the board or on a piece of chart paper. Ask students to point out the first vowels in *farm* and *farmer.* Explain that they do not hear a long or short vowel sound; instead, they hear the letter r say its name. Point out that some vowels are r-controlled because the letter r (sometimes called bossy r) makes the vowel sound different. Ask students what little word they can find in both words (*arm*). Then, ask them to think of other words that contain the /ar/ sound such as *harm, charm, barn, part, smart, cart, tart,* and *garden.* Provide alphabet cards (pages 159-160) and ask students to put the cards in the correct order to spell the /ar/ words they list. Display the words on a pocket chart. As students read the story, have them add any words that they find. They should be able to find *barn* and *party.* Draw a big picture of a barn and have students write the ar words on cards that you can tape to the barn, or write the words directly on the barn. On the barn, add the title "AR Words."

Post-reading Activity: Explain that there are many different types of animals on a farm. Have students share the names of animals they think might live on a farm. Provide alphabet cards (pages 159-160). Have each student select a card and draw a farm animal whose name begins with the letter she selected. (Provide some letters more than once, and eliminate difficult letters like x and q.) Ask each student to label her picture with the letter of the alphabet and the name of the animal, and write a simple sentence about the animal. When students have finished their drawings, ask students to stand in line with their pictures in the correct alphabetical order. Collect the pictures and create a class book entitled *Alphabetic Farm Animals.*

Name_____ Date _____

Use this with the phonics pre-reading activity. Give two reproducibles to each student. Have students cut out the flower pattern on this page and use it to create two ou and ow flowers. Ask them to list words on the petals of one flower that contain the sound of ou/ow as in the word *grow*. Have them list words on the petals of the other flower that contain the sound of ou/ow as in *flower.*

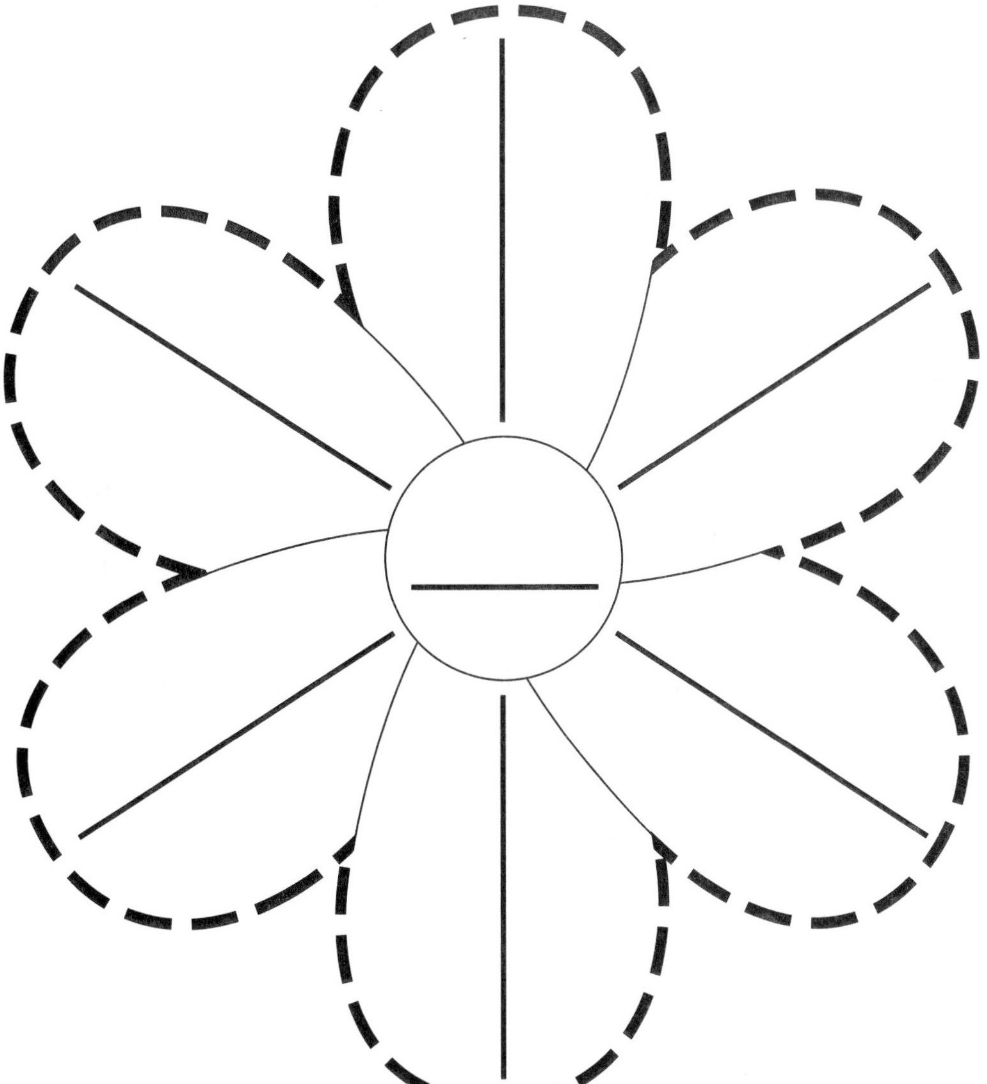

Vocabulary Activities
for *Click, Clack, Moo: Cows That Type*

Pre-reading Activity: Write the following words on a piece of chart paper: *impatient, problem, impossible, electric, blankets, typewriter, furious, neutral, ultimatum, emergency, exchange.* Talk about each word. Ask students to try to figure out the pronunciation of each word by looking for smaller base words. Use each word in a sentence for them and ask them to use the sentences to guess the meanings of the words. List the definition next to each word on the chart. Remind students to refer to the chart as you read the story if they aren't sure of the meanings of the sentences.

During-reading Activity: Sometimes, it is easier for students to remember the definition of a word if you assign a motion to the word. Read the story to students. Ask students to clap or click their fingers to "alert" you when you read one of the words from the vocabulary chart in the pre-reading activity. Once they alert you, have them help you put a motion to the word. For example, for the word *impatient*, have them tap their feet. For the word *problem*, have them put index fingers to their foreheads. For *typewriter*, have students pretend to type. For the word *impossible*, have them throw their hands above their heads. For *ultimatum*, have them point their fingers and shake them. Once you have determined a motion for each word, have students reread the story with you, but this time, when you come to a vocabulary word, only give the motion and allow students to identify the word by watching your motion and looking at the word in context. Have them say the word and repeat the motion.

Post-reading Activity: Throughout the story, the phrase "Click, clack, moo" is repeated. At the end of the story, the phrase changes to "Click, clack, quack" because the ducks ask Farmer Brown for a diving board. Explain that some words, like *moo* and *quack*, sound like the sounds that animals make. Use the Animal Sounds reproducible (page 33) to create more characters for the book and practice writing words that represent the animals' sounds. Have each student select an animal and draw a picture of it. Then, ask him to fill in the speech bubble to finish the phrases "Click, clack _____! Click, clack _____! Clickety, clack _____!" with the correct animal sound. See how many animal sounds students can come up with. Help them spell the harder ones. Add the new characters to the bulletin board containing the flowers and barn from the phonics pre- and during-reading activities.

Name_____ Date _____

Choose a new animal to use the typewriter. Draw a picture of the animal. Then, write the sound that your animal makes in the blanks.

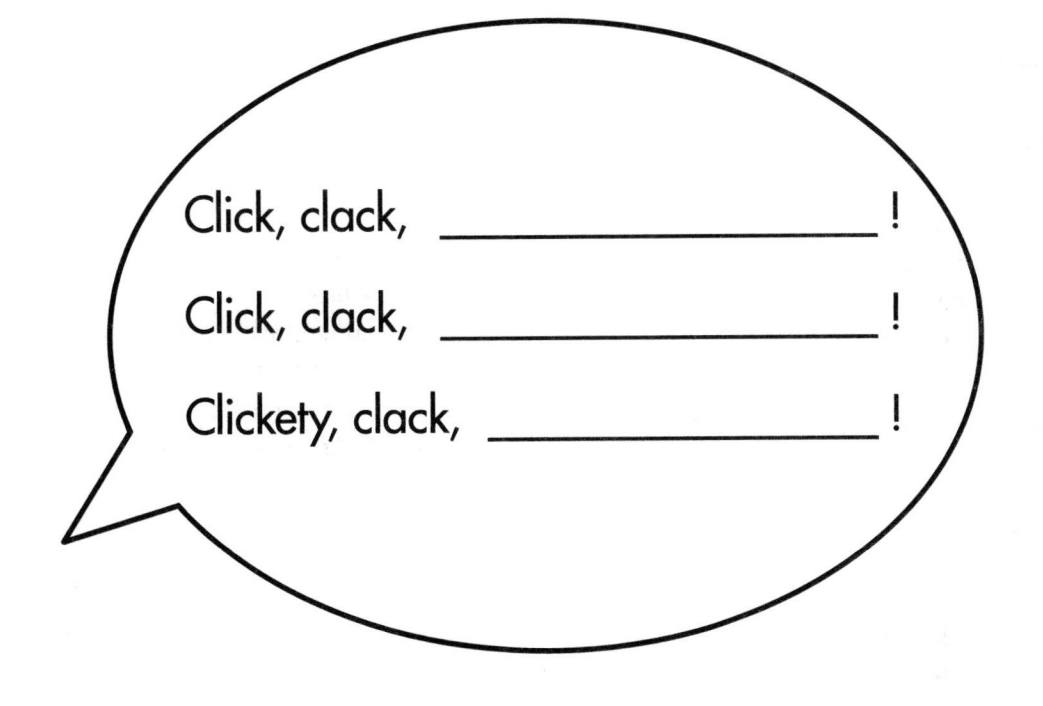

Click, clack, _____ !

Click, clack, _____ !

Clickety, clack, _____ !

Fluency Activities
for *Click, Clack, Moo: Cows That Type*

Pre-reading Activity: Use singing to help students become more fluent. Students will have fun singing the song "Old MacDonald." Write the song lyrics on a large piece of chart paper. Have students read the song using the correct rhythm. Then, have them follow along and sing the song as you point to the words. Sing the traditional animals first, then add some more unusual ones. Point to a student and have him come up with a silly animal and its sounds. For example, use students' responses to sing in this pattern:

"Old MacDonald had a farm, e-i-e-i-o!
And on this farm he had a _____ (student names animal), e-i-e-i-o!
With a _____ _____ (student makes noise) here and a _____ _____ (class makes noise) there.
Here a _____, there a _____, everywhere a _____ _____!
Old MacDonald had a farm, e-i-e-i-o!"

During-reading Activity: Before reading the story, ask students to try to determine how Farmer Brown is feeling by the way your voice sounds as you read his statements. Ask if they can understand how the animals are feeling by the way your voice sounds as you read their notes in the story. (You may want to tell students that when reading correspondence or e-mail, it can be hard to tell how the writer is feeling.) Explain that Farmer Brown and the animals display many different emotions. Remind students that when they read aloud, they should express these emotions in their voices. As you read the book, pause to discuss how the characters are feeling. If students have difficulty understanding the emotions, model for them the different sentences and phrases that show the farmers' impatience and anger and the cows' stubbornness. Then, reread the story as a class and assign students to three groups. Have one group repeat the moo phrases, another group pretend to be Farmer Brown, and a third group read all of the notes. Control the flow of the story by serving as narrator. During the reading, pause to talk about how each group shows emotion with their voices.

Post-reading Activity: Provide multiple copies of the book and have students read the story together to practice fluency. Allow them to take turns reading different pages, but ask that they repeat the *click, clack* phrases and all of the notes together. After students are familiar with the story, assign students different roles and put on a radio show. Stress that in radio, it is essential not to stumble over words because there are no visual cues. Assign a reader or readers to each of the following parts: Farmer Brown, cows, duck, narrator. Then, assign different students to do sound effects. Refer to the Sound Effects reproducible (page 35) for a list of possible sounds and how to make them. Stand at the front of the classroom and cue readers and noisemakers to read and "act out" the text. Rehearse several times, then record the show. Wait several days, then turn down the lights and play the recording as a treat.

Sound Effects
fluency reproducible for
Click, Clack, Moo: Cows That Type

Use the sound effects listed below to add interest to your *Click, Clack, Moo* radio show. Also, consider having students bring in toys that make animal sounds to make sounds for the cows, chickens, and duck.

• When the text mentions typing, type on a keyboard. A computer keyboard will work, but an old-fashioned typewriter sounds better and will be more true to the story.

• When the cows are mentioned, turn over a cow noisemaker (or moo like a cow).

• When the chickens are mentioned, shake the cow noisemaker up and down to create a short and high-pitched sound.

• When the ducks are mentioned, quack on a kazoo (or quack like a duck).

• When the farmer walks to the barn, tap shoes or boots on a table in a walking motion to make footsteps. Or, have a student push her hands in a flat pan of gelatin to sound like walking through mud. Or, squeeze a box of cornstarch to sound like the farmer is walking through snow. (It is cold out there, after all!)

• When the ducks get their diving board at the end of the book, drop a wooden block into a half-full pitcher of water.

Comprehension Activities
for *Click, Clack, Moo: Cows That Type*

Pre-reading Activity: Initiate a lesson about fact and fiction. Inform students that *Click Clack Moo: Cows That Type* is a very unusual story about cows. Draw a large picture of a cow on bulletin board paper and attach it to a wall or bulletin board. Have students tell everything they know about cows. List correct statements on the cow. Explain that they just helped you list true statements which are called *facts*. Next, show them the cover of the book. Introduce the title, author, and illustrator. Ask them to look carefully at the illustration to determine what the cows are doing. Explain that the cows are typing and since cows can't really type this part is not true, or *fiction*. Give examples of fiction, then explain that *Click Clack Moo: Cows That Type* is fictional because there are a number of events in the story that cannot happen in real life. Repeat some facts and then some sentences that are fictional. Have students identify which are facts and which are fiction, and tell why. Look at the illustrations in the book and ask students to point out things they think could be facts and other things they think are fiction. To reinforce the concepts, play a game called Fact or Fiction. Create a second chart titled "Animals Can't ____." Assign each student an animal name. Have the student research, then report to the class three facts and one fictional statement about the animal. Allow classmates to identify the fictional statement and explain why it is not true. Let the student who correctly identifies the fictional statement be the next to present.

During-reading Activity: On a piece of chart paper or on the board, write the following column headings: *Title, Author, Illustrator, Characters, Setting, Problems,* and *Solutions*. Discuss the definition of each word. As you read the story, ask questions about the different headings and have students help you fill in the chart. Be sure to show them where in the book they can find the author and illustrator. You may want to display the chart in the classroom and use it to compare and contrast future books. For example, challenge students to find and read books by the same author or illustrator. Or, read another book about cows or a farmer and point out to students that they have listed similar characters under the *Characters* heading for *Click, Clack, Moo: Cows That Type*. If the chart is used and displayed for a long period of time, it will help students form a picture of the knowledge they have gained through their reading.

Post-reading Activity: Remind students that the problems in *Click Clack Moo: Cows That Type* were solved when the animals and Farmer Brown wrote notes to each other. Help students make a list of farm animals, then brainstorm things these new animals might ask Farmer Brown to get for them. Explain that before they can suggest something for the animals on the list, they must have a reason why the particular animal might want the requested item. For example, why do they think the ducks asked for a diving board? Give each student a copy of the What Animals Want reproducible (page 37). Have each student pretend to be one of the animals writing to Farmer Brown to ask for what she wants, and why she needs or wants it. Collect the notes and redistribute them. Then, ask each student to pretend she is Farmer Brown and write a note on the back of the paper to the animal about the request she made. Is it granted? Why or why not?

What Animals Want

comprehension reproducible for
Click, Clack, Moo: Cows That Type

Name_____ Date _____

Pretend you are an animal on the farm. Use the lines below to write a letter to Farmer Brown to ask for something. When you get a classmate's letter, answer it on the back of the page as if you are Farmer Brown. Will you say yes or no? Why?

_____

_____

_____

_____

_____

_____

_____

_____

 _____

The FOOT BOOK
by Dr. Seuss

(Random House, 1968)

This classic Dr. Seuss story describes the different feet a character observes as he takes a walk. The simple, repetitious text can be used to initiate lessons on special vowel configurations, antonyms, and directional words.

Related books: *Fox in Socks* by Dr. Seuss (Random House, 1965); *One Fish Two Fish Red Fish Blue Fish* by Dr. Seuss (Random House, 1960)

Phonemic Awareness Activities
for *The Foot Book*

Pre-reading Activity: Enlarge the cards on the Foot and Feet reproducible (page 39). Show students pictures of the foot and feet. Ask students to say the words and identify the sounds that are different in each. Show the other cards with the following pictures: *book, football, hood, hook, bee, knee, leaf, peach.* Have students say the picture names. Then, shuffle the cards and have students take turns selecting cards to share with the class. Students should say the picture names and repeat the matching sounds (/oo/ or long /e/). Have them place the cards in two separate piles: one for names containing the /oo/ sound and another for names containing the long /e/ sound. Place these cards in a center where students can work in pairs to review these sounds.

During-reading Activity: Read *The Foot Book* aloud. Point out that students will hear the /oo/ and the long /e/ sounds in words throughout the story. As you read the story, have students stamp one foot once if they hear /oo/ and stamp both feet twice if they hear long /e/ in a word. Have them repeat /oo/ or long /e/ and the word after making the motions.

Post-reading Activity: Before conducting this activity, use a marker to trace around each of your bare feet to make left and right foot patterns. Make about 15 copies of the feet. Leave ten together for long /e/ and cut apart five for /oo/. On the patterns, glue or draw pictures of things with names that contain an /oo/ or long /e/ sound as in the words *foot* and *feet*. Laminate the footprints. Play a game called "Tiptoe Around the Room." Tape the footprints to the floor close enough for students to walk on them. As they take turns stepping on each footprint, have students look at each picture, say its name, and identify the vowel sound. To finish the game, students must be able to correctly identify each sound and picture word on the path around the room. To challenge more advanced students, add footprints containing pictures with other vowel sounds. In order to finish this game, students must avoid stepping on footprints that do not have pictures containing the /oo/ and long /e/ sounds.

Name_____ Date _____

Cut out the cards. Sort the pictures into two piles. One pile should have words that have the /oo/ sound, like *foot*. The other pile should have words that have the long /e/ sound, like *feet*.

foot

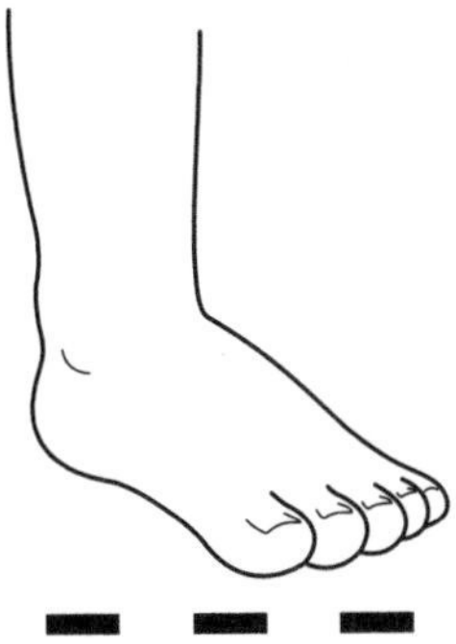

feet

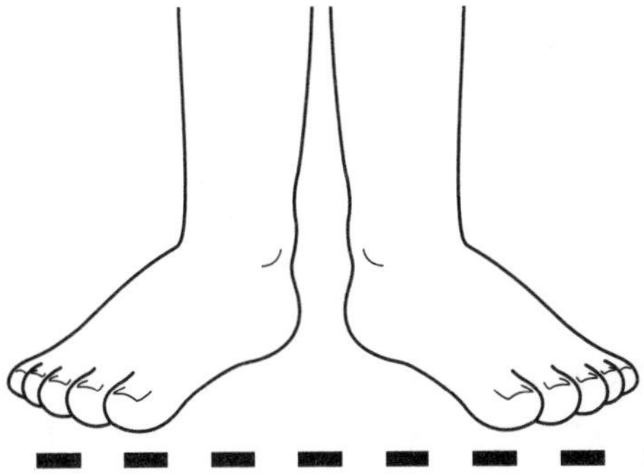

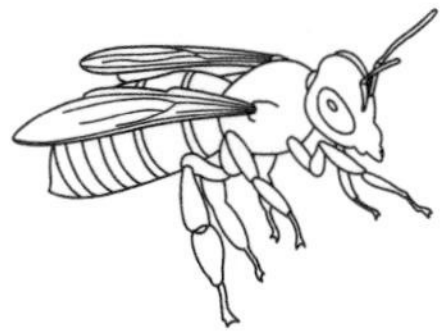

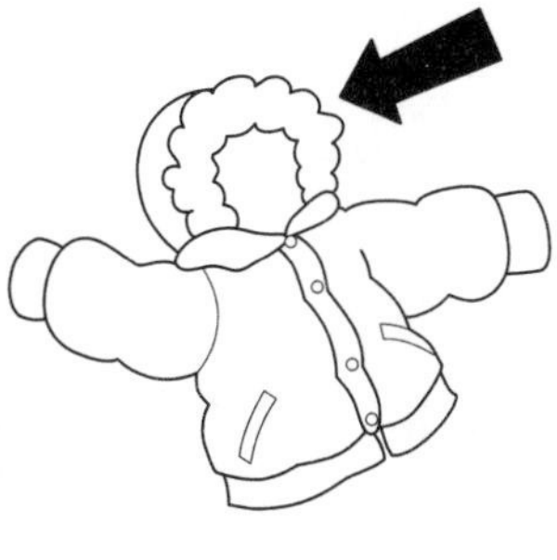

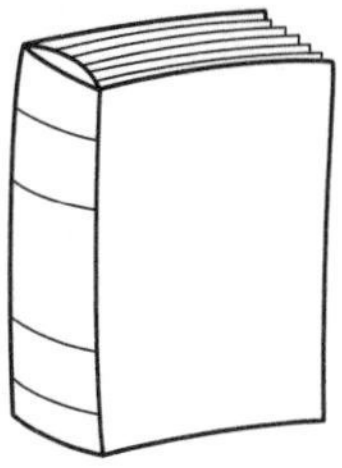

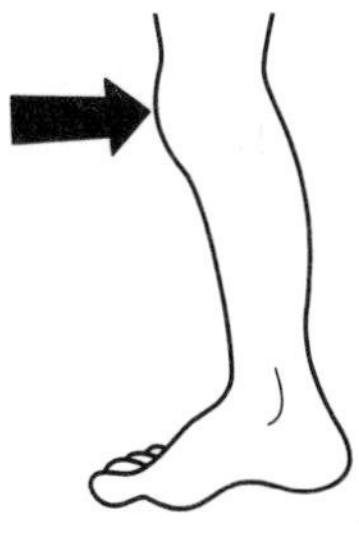

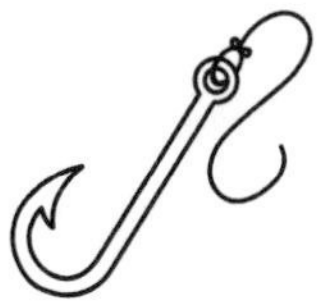

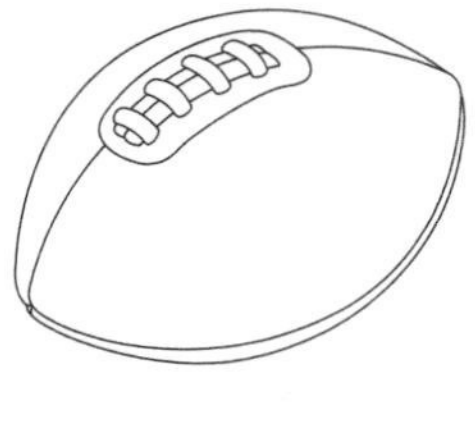

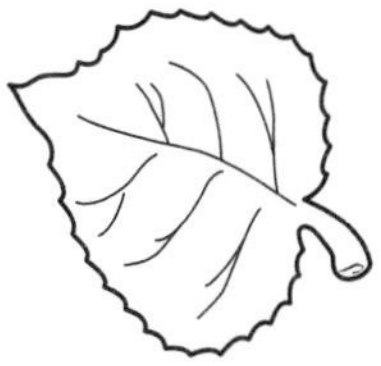

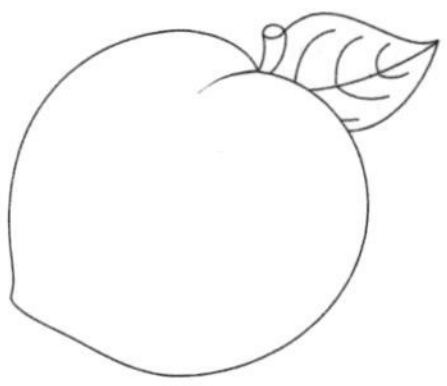

Phonics Activities
for *The Foot Book*

Pre-reading Activity: To prepare for this lesson, write *Short /i/ Sound* at the top of a piece of chart paper. Explain that there are words containing the short /i/ sound throughout the book. Provide multiple copies of *The Foot Book*. Have students work in pairs or groups to search for and write down words with the short /i/ sound. Once all students have had a chance to search the book, ask the whole class to help you fill in the chart. Students should be able to find *trick, sick, pig, big, quick, in,* and *his.* Explain to students that some of these words are in families together. Ask them to match the two word family pairs from the list. They should be able to identify *trick/sick* and *pig/big.* Direct students to use the Families that Have a Short /i/ reproducible (page 41) to think of other words that end with ick or ig. Have them add the words to the appropriate columns on their pages.

During-reading Activity: Have each student take off his shoes and socks and wiggle his toes. Ask, "What sound do you hear at the beginning of the word *wiggle* (short /i/)?" Have students put one sock and shoe on again, and let students who have sneakers tie the laces. Ask, "What sound do you hear in the word *tie* (long /i/)?" Point out to students that besides words containing the short /i/ sound, the book also contains words that contain the letter i that makes the long /i/ sound as in *tie.* As you read the book aloud, ask students to wiggle their toes each time they hear a word with either a short /i/ sound, and wiggle their shoes when they hear a word with the long /i/ sound. Have them repeat each word they hear and call out either "long i" or "short i" to identify which sound the letter i makes in each word. (If students identify the word *dry,* explain that sometimes the letter y has the same sound as long /i/.)

Post-reading Activity: Point out the word *book* in the title. Inform students that this word can be used to make new words. Write each letter in the word *book* on an index card and place the letters in a pocket chart. Remove the b and ask students to say the sound that the remaining letters make when blended together (ook). Replace the letter b with the letter c and say the word *cook.* Inform students that they can make other words by continuing to replace just the first letter. Let them know that the words they can form in this manner are part of the ook word family. Have students work in pairs or small groups to create new words containing ook. They can practice making the words using letter cards or plastic letters. Have them write the words that they create and share them with the class later. Extend this activity by giving students other words in the book, such as *right* and *feet,* and asking them to follow the same process to create other word families.

Families that Have a Short /i/
phonics reproducible for
The Foot Book
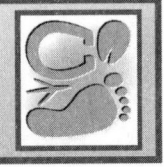

Name_____   Date_____

Think of more words that end in ick or ig. Write them on this chart.

ick	ig
_____	_____
_____	_____
_____	_____
_____	_____
_____	_____
_____	_____
_____	_____

_ick   _ig

Vocabulary Activities
for *The Foot Book*

Pre-reading Activity: Explain to students that many of the words in this story are associated with each other because they are *antonyms*. Antonyms are words that have opposite meanings. Point out that on the first page, the opposites *left* and *right* are listed. Have students work in pairs using multiple copies of the book to discover and record the sets of antonyms throughout the text. They should be able to find *left/right*, *morning/night*, *wet/dry*, *high/low*, *front/back*, *slow/quick*, *up/down*, *his/her*, and *small/big*.

During-reading Activity: Review the antonyms found by students during the pre-reading activity. As you reread the story, have students say the opposite response to what you say. For example, if you say, "Left foot, left foot," they should respond with "Right foot, right foot." There are at least seven additional words in the story that have antonyms not mentioned in the text. Challenge students to find them and provide their opposites: *his/her*, *here/there*, *over/under*, *on/off*, *come/go*, *in/out*, and *black/white*. Once students have completed these activities, distribute the Opposite Socks reproducible (page 43). Ask each student to lightly color both sock patterns so that they match. Assign each student a different antonym pair and have her write one word on each sock. Either repeat antonyms used in the story or challenge students with additional words you choose that have antonyms but do not appear in the text. Some examples are *fat/thin*, *tall/short*, *happy/sad*, *day/night*, *stop/go*, *open/close*, and *yes/no*. Use the finished socks to create a bulletin board by using clothespins to attach them in random order. Challenge students to match antonyms and hang them correctly from a string each day. Rearrange them at the end of each day. Title the bulletin board "Start Off on the Right Foot with Opposites."

Post-reading Activity: Before this activity, have students trace their feet and cut out the patterns. Some of the antonyms identified above are also *directional words*. Explain what directional words are. Point out a pair and ask students to find others in the story. As they find them, write them on the footprint cutouts, then set them aside. Since directional words are often a hard concept for young students to master, help them understand the concept better by playing a game of Simon Says. Say, "Simon says to put your hand *on* your head. Simon says to stoop *down* low. Jump *up* in the air." Tell students to remember only to do what Simon says! After using the game to remind students about the purpose and definitions of directional words, let them demonstrate their understanding of the concept. Assign students to small groups. Give each group a footprint with a directional word. Ask the group members to agree on a place in the room to tape the footprint so that its meaning is clear. For example, they might tape a footprint with the word *under* below the board. Review the placement of the footprints, and have volunteers name the words on the feet and tell how their placement in the classroom relates to the directional words written on them.

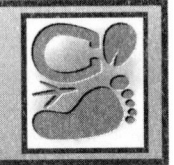

Name_____ Date _____

Lightly color the two socks below so that they match. On the lines in the foot sections, write the antonyms your teacher assigns. Then, cut out the socks.

Fluency Activities
for *The Foot Book*

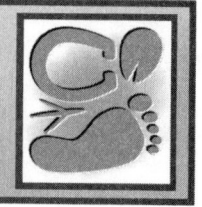

Pre-reading Activity: Explain to students that reading should not be slow and choppy. It should be smooth and flow much the same way that people normally speak when they have a conversation. Purchase a premade recording of *The Foot Book* or record yourself or a parent volunteer reading the book. Let students follow along with the book silently and then aloud. This will help them read with appropriate pace and rhythm rather than word-by-word. Put the recording at a center for students to use for independent practice.

During-reading Activity: Once students have practiced oral reading with the recording, ask them to listen as you model the manner in which the story should be read. Have them clap the rhythm as you read. Continue until students can read the story fluently with you without clapping. Next, give each student a copy of the My Hands and Feet reproducible (page 45). After reading the poem aloud once, read it again while students clap the rhythm. Then, have them work in pairs until they can read the poem fluently without clapping. After students have mastered the reading, have them look carefully at the last stanza of the poem. Help them recognize what is different about that stanza (it is longer, it is written in complete sentences, neither *hands* nor *feet* begins the first line, and there is an extra, unstressed syllable at the beginning of each line) and what is the same (it is still read in the same rhythm, although one line of the last stanza has the same number of stressed beats as two lines of the previous stanzas).

Post-reading Activity: Create a reading center for students by providing an assortment of easy-to-read Dr. Seuss books, along with other rhyming books. Use index cards to create a deck of Fluency is Fun cards. Program the cards with different actions such as clapping, tapping fingers, tapping feet, tapping pencils together, snapping fingers, waving hands, or nodding heads. Pair students and let each pair select a card and decide which student will provide motion and which will read. Have each pair begin this exercise letting one student read while the other student taps out the rhythm of the page. Periodically, ask students to switch roles and continue to practice. Inform students that when they have mastered books and can read them smoothly, they will present them to the class. Have students take turns reading or providing motion. If they can handle performing more advanced actions, let students perform actions such as directing a band, hammering a nail, typing an imaginary typewriter, etc, while their classmates guess the new actions.

My Hands and Feet

fluency reproducible for
The Foot Book

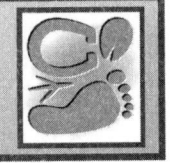

Name _____ Date _____

Work in pairs. Read the poem aloud with your partner, clapping to the rhythm of the poem. Practice until you can read it fluently.

My Hands and Feet

Hands that write
And hands that wiggle,
Hands held tight
And hands that jiggle!

Hands that shake
And hands that clap
Hands that bake
And hands that snap.

Feet that prance
And feet that jump,
Feet that dance
And feet that bump.

Feet that skip
And feet that hop,
Feet that trip
And feet that stop.

I use my hands to tie my shoes.
I use my feet to walk the street.
My hands and feet are mine to use.
Hands and feet are really neat!

Comprehension Activities
for *The Foot Book*

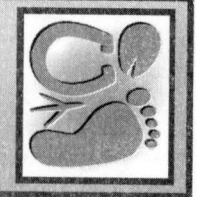

re-reading Activity: Introduce *The Foot Book* to students by having them look at the picture on the cover. Ask them to focus on the character and what he is pointing to (his foot). Next, ask them to read the title. Ask, "What might this story be about?" Students will probably tell you the book is about a foot. Ask, "What are feet? What has them? Who has them? What do they look like? Are all feet the same?" As you are conducting the discussion, draw an outline of a footprint on the board. Ask students to give examples of things that have feet. As they offer suggestions, list them on the board. Review all of the suggestions and ask them to predict which ones they might see in the book. Next, have them look at the illustrations on each page to see if their predictions were correct. Place stars next to the predictions that matched illustrations in the story.

uring-reading Activity: Many students will have already read this book, so have them read along with you. Stop periodically to ask questions about the various feet the character sees on his walk. Were they different sizes, shapes, colors, or numbers? Although the setting appears ambiguous, ask students to observe the different illustrations and consider where his walk has taken him to see the different types of feet. Ask students to look at each other's feet (with shoes on) to see how many different shapes, sizes, and colors they have. Then, play a classification game. Have students stand in groups according to shoe color. Discuss the idea of classification and ask students for other ways to group their shoes such as shape or size. Let students use the Foot Sort reproducible (page 47) to make bar graphs of the results of the shoe color classification. You may also want to do this activity before reading, and add characters' feet to the graph as you read about them in the story. To extend the activity, adjust the graph to track other feet characteristics.

ost-reading Activity: Before initiating this activity, gather a long sheet of bulletin board paper, different colors of tempera paint, shallow containers to hold the paint, buckets of soapy water, clean water, and towels. Explain to students that you would like to take them on an imaginary, adventurous walk, but there is a catch. Inform them that they will let their hands do the walking. Have students take turns carefully placing their hands into containers of their favorite colors of paint. Students should then press their hands on the bulletin board paper. Let it dry overnight. The next day, have students write stories about where their hands are going. Attach the stories to the bulletin board paper near each student's pair of hands.

Name_____ Date _____

Use the bar graph below to sort the shoes in your class by color.

Shoe Colors in _____'s Class

10
9
8
7
6
5
4
3
2
1
0

number of students

white pink red orange yellow green blue purple brown black multi

colors

The Grouchy Ladybug

by Eric Carle

(HarperCollins, 1977)

The Grouchy Ladybug is primarily about manners and time. The grouchy ladybug is not the most gracious bug in the world. It doesn't share and has an inflated ego. It picks a fight with every creature it meets until finally it meets its match—a huge whale who won't dignify the ladybug's question with an answer. The obvious curriculum connection is teaching manners. A little clock in the top left corner of several pages can be used to teach time. Since each animal that the ladybug meets is larger than the last, this book can also help teach the concepts of size and shape. Because this is a circular story, students can also create their own innovations to tell a similar story.

Related books: *Are You a Ladybug?* by Judy Allen and Tudor Humphries (Larousse Kingfisher Chambers, 2000); *The Very Lazy Ladybug* by Isobel Finn (Tiger Tales, 2003)

Phonemic Awareness Activities
for *The Grouchy Ladybug*

Pre-reading Activity: The main character in the story is a ladybug. Ask students to repeat the base word *bug.* Inform them that they can create words that sound like *bug* by replacing the /b/ sound. Give them an example such as *rug.* First, say ug, then say the /r/ and /ug/ sounds and blend them together to make *rug.* Ask students to think of other words that they can say that end in ug. Accept nonsense words but then ask students to identify the real words. Encourage them to use blends and digraphs, not just single sounds, to create words like *slug* and *shrug.*

During-reading Activity: This story begins at night. Ask students to say the word *night.* What do they hear when they remove the letter n? Have them repeat the sound ight. Explain that other initial sounds can be added to ight to make new words. Have them say other words that sound like *night* and *right,* then listen for *night* and *right* on the first two pages. Read the third page of the story and ask if they hear another word that sounds like *night* and *right* (*fight*). Explain that *fight* will be repeated. Make listening for these words a silly activity. Have a student stand near the light switch. When you read the word *fight* or another word that rhymes with *night,* let that student turn off the lights briefly to make it "night" in the classroom. Let pairs practice this activity at a center with a flashlight.

Post-reading Activity: Do this activity with 12 students at a time. Ask students to identify each animal that the ladybug meets in its travels. Cut out the cards on the Ladybug Friends reproducible (page 49) and place them in a bag. Have each student select a card, say the name of the animal, and identify its initial sound. Have him find something else in the room that begins with the same sound and place the card by the object.

Ladybug Friends

phonemic awareness reproducible for
The Grouchy Ladybug

Name_____ Date _____

Use the cards below with the phonemic awareness post-reading activity to challenge students to find objects that have the same initial sounds as the names of the animals. See the book or answer key for picture names.

Phonics Activities
for *The Grouchy Ladybug*

 re-reading Activity: Write the words *if, it's,* and *big* on the board. Have students say each word and listen for the vowel sound. Ask, "What is the vowel sound in each of these words?" Students should be able to recognize the short /i/ sound. Generate a list of words that have the short /i/ sound. Explain to students that when a word or syllable contains a short vowel and is followed by a consonant, the word or syllable is considered a *closed syllable*. Ask students to read the story in pairs. As they read the story, challenge them to find and list words containing the letter i. Then, ask them to identify all of the words containing closed syllables with short /i/ sounds. Some of the words students should find include *insist, aphid, in, big, pick,* and *itself.*

uring-reading Activity: Students will be very curious about the whale in the story because it doesn't respond to the grouchy ladybug when different parts of its body are asked to fight. As you read the book, pause when you reach the part about the whale, write the word *whale* on the board and ask students to read it. Tell them that the /wh/ sound is special; it is called a *consonant digraph*. Say the sound with them. (Note that some regional dialects and phonics programs pronounce this digraph like the /w/ sound; adjust the lesson accordingly.) Have students brainstorm a list of other words that begin with wh. Draw a picture of a whale and write the list on it. Explain that there are other letters that, when combined, have special sounds. Write *shark, cheese,* and *three* on the board. Ask students to say the words. Direct them to listen to the sound that the first two letters in each word make when combined. Allow students to think of other sh, ch, and th words and list them. List sh words on a picture of a shark, ch words on a picture of a cheese wedge, and th words on a number three. (Note: There are actually two sounds associated with th. There is voiced /th/ as in *there*, which vibrates the vocal cords, and unvoiced /th/ as in *thing*, which does not.) As you read through the story, ask students to point out words that contain consonant digraphs. Point out that there is a /ch/ sound in *grouchy* to get them started.

ost-reading Activity: After reading the story, have students create pull-through cards to practice saying and recognizing words that end in ug and ale. Explain that *ladybug* ends in ug and *whale* ends in ale. Give each student an enlarged copy of the Words with UG and ALE reproducible (page 51) to cut out, assemble, and color. Use the words from the reproducible as spelling words or add them to a word wall. You may also want to laminate a copy of the pieces for use at a center.

Name_____ Date _____

Cut out the ladybug, the whale, and the two strips. Cut two slits on each animal. Lace the strips of paper through the slits on the patterns, and create new words by sliding the strips up and down.

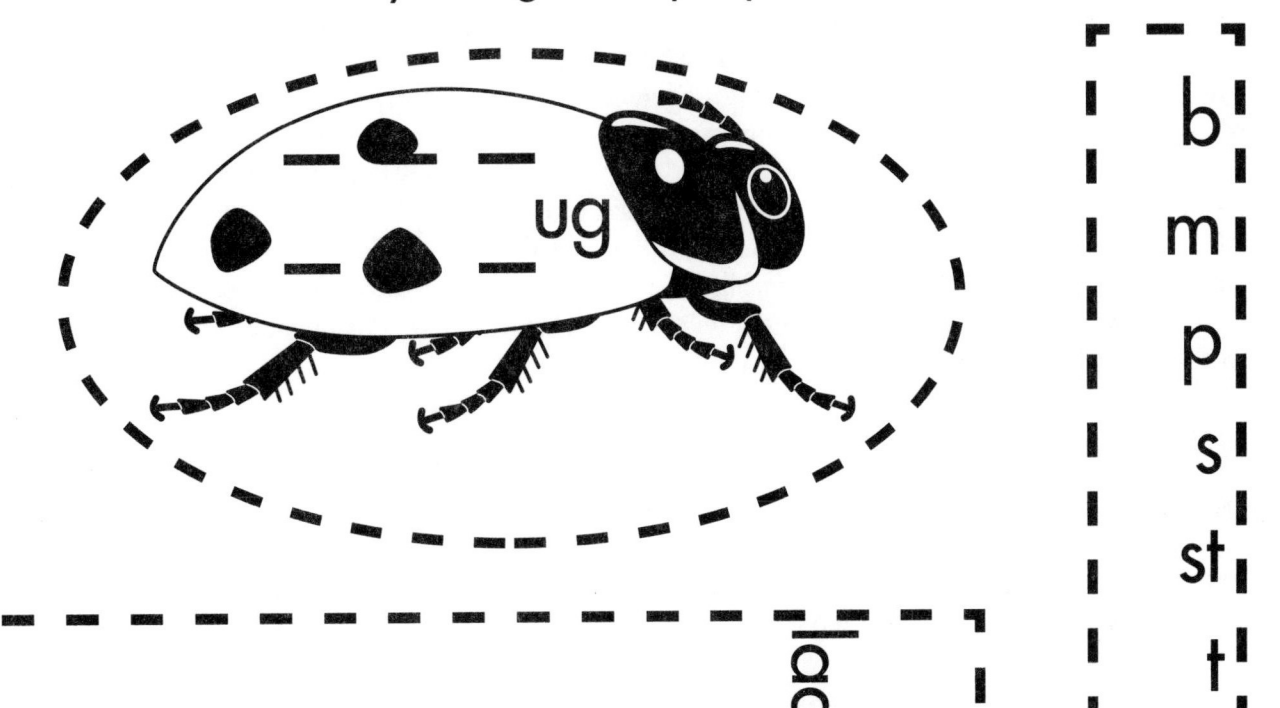

_ug

b
m
p
s
st
t
wh

t su pl m h p ladyb

ale

Vocabulary Activities
for *The Grouchy Ladybug*

**P**re-reading Activity: Look through the book with students. Explain to them that there are many hard words in the book. The hard words are the names of different animals that the grouchy ladybug talks to as it travels. Point out the animal in each illustration. Ask students if they know the name of each. If they don't guess correctly, give them the names and point them out in the text (*yellow jacket, stag beetle, praying mantis, sparrow, lobster, skunk, boa constrictor, hyena, gorilla, rhinoceros, elephant, whale, fireflies*). Use index cards to create a set of name cards for the animal names. Place them in a bag. Have each student pick a card out of the bag. Enlarge the picture cards from the Ladybug Friends reproducible (page 49) and place them in a pocket chart or on the ledge of the board. Ask students to look at the words on the cards they selected from the bag. If they don't know the words, ask them to look for smaller words or "chunks" they recognize to help them figure out the words. You may want them to work in pairs. As you point to each animal picture, have students look at their cards to see who has the match. Have each student place her matching card next to the correct picture. Continue until all matches have been made. Then, review the animal names. Have students point to the names in the text while looking at the illustrations.

During-reading Activity: Create a sentence strip for each phrase that demonstrates the action of an animal the grouchy ladybug meets. For example, for the yellow jacket, write *showing its stinger.* Explain to students that each animal does something in response to the ladybug's question, "Do you want to fight?" Show the sentence strips to students. Ask them to help you read the different phrases. As you read the story together, ask students to listen for the phrases and see who says each one. As you read each phrase, let a volunteer put it in the pocket chart next to the name cards and pictures you used in the vocabulary pre-reading activity. Have students read each phrase together.

Post-reading Activity: Encourage students to help you retell the story by looking at the illustrations. Let a few students pretend to be animals. Guide the story by reading the narrator's part. Ask the different "animals" to use the phrases on the sentence strips and make motions to show the actions of the animals as they repeat the phrase, "If you insist." Make sure students can identify the ladybug's question to each animal and the answer given in each case with the exception of the whale. Use the Name That Action! reproducible (page 53) to check students' knowledge of the names of the animals and the actions in the story.

Name_____ Date _____

The grouchy ladybug asks different creatures if they want to fight.
Each one answers with an action. Write the name of each animal's
action on the line beneath it.

_____

_____

_____

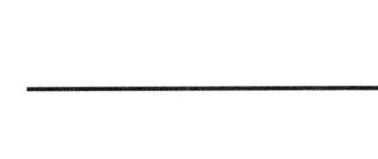

_____   _____

_____   _____   _____

_____

Fluency Activities
for *The Grouchy Ladybug*

Pre-reading Activity: Use the question the ladybug asks to combine fluency practice with humor. Tell students that it isn't appropriate to ask, "Do you want to fight?" But, the grouchy ladybug does it and never gets the answer it wants. Explain that even though the ladybug probably sounded very grouchy when asking that question, there are many ways to ask it that can be funny. Have one student come to the front of the classroom. Whisper a silly scenario to her such as "You are being tickled by a hundred feathers!" Have her imagine how she would sound then have her ask, "Do you want to fight?" Have students repeat the question in the same manner as the volunteer, then try to guess what the scenario might be. Other possible scenarios might include being underwater, being very cold, jumping on a trampoline, listening to very sad music, riding a galloping horse, etc.

During-reading Activity: Have students take on the roles of different animals in the story. Remind them that people use different intonations when asking questions than when making statements. The tone of a question is one of curiosity, so the speaker's voice rises at the end. But, a person would use an explanatory tone when responding to a question. Remind students that the ladybug is grouchy—how would it respond to each animal it meets? Talk about the sizes of the different animals. Students should notice that the animals start out very small and get bigger each time one is introduced. Explain to them that the animals' voices might get louder or deeper because of this. Have students practice using louder and deeper voices as the animals become larger. As you read the end of the story (when the whale slaps the grouchy ladybug back to land), ask, "How might the ladybug's tone of voice change when it speaks to the other ladybug?" Have students practice the story with you. Then, have students sit in a circle. Give each student a card that identifies him as one of the animals. Select one student to be the ladybug. Starting with the friendly ladybug, have the "ladybug" visit each animal and retell the story. Have students stand to answer and make the motions of the animals as they respond. (If you have too many students, make some students timekeepers to change the time before the grouchy ladybug can visit the next animal.) Make sure students use the correct intonations for their responses. Ask them to think of another set of animals that the grouchy ladybug can visit and challenge to fight. List the animals on the board. Have students number them in order from the smallest to the largest animal. Talk about what action each animal might make as it replies, "If you insist," to the ladybug. Have students tell the story again, but this time as other animals. Make sure they use the correct intonations for the new animals.

Post-reading Activity: Build on the animal voices from the during-reading activity. Give each student a copy of the What Do I Sound Like? reproducible (page 55). Tell her to cut out the animal wheel. Give each student a paper dessert plate. Instruct her to cut a pie-shaped piece out of the dessert plate. The wedge should be about an inch wide at the edge. Then, have students attach the plates on top of the animal wheels with paper fasteners. Again, discuss how this story would sound if the whale were reading it. Ask, "Would it be in a small, quiet voice? How about if a hyena were reading it? Do hyenas sound serious?" Pair students with reading partners. Let each student turn to an animal and read to his partner in that animal's "voice" without revealing what animal she chose. Let each partner guess the animal by her voice. After each student has had a turn, have students switch partners and select new animals.

What Do I Sound like?

fluency reproducible for
The Grouchy Ladybug

Name_____ Date _____

Cut out the animal wheel. Trace the wheel on another sheet of paper and cut it out. Your teacher will tell you how to assemble your wheels and play a reading game.

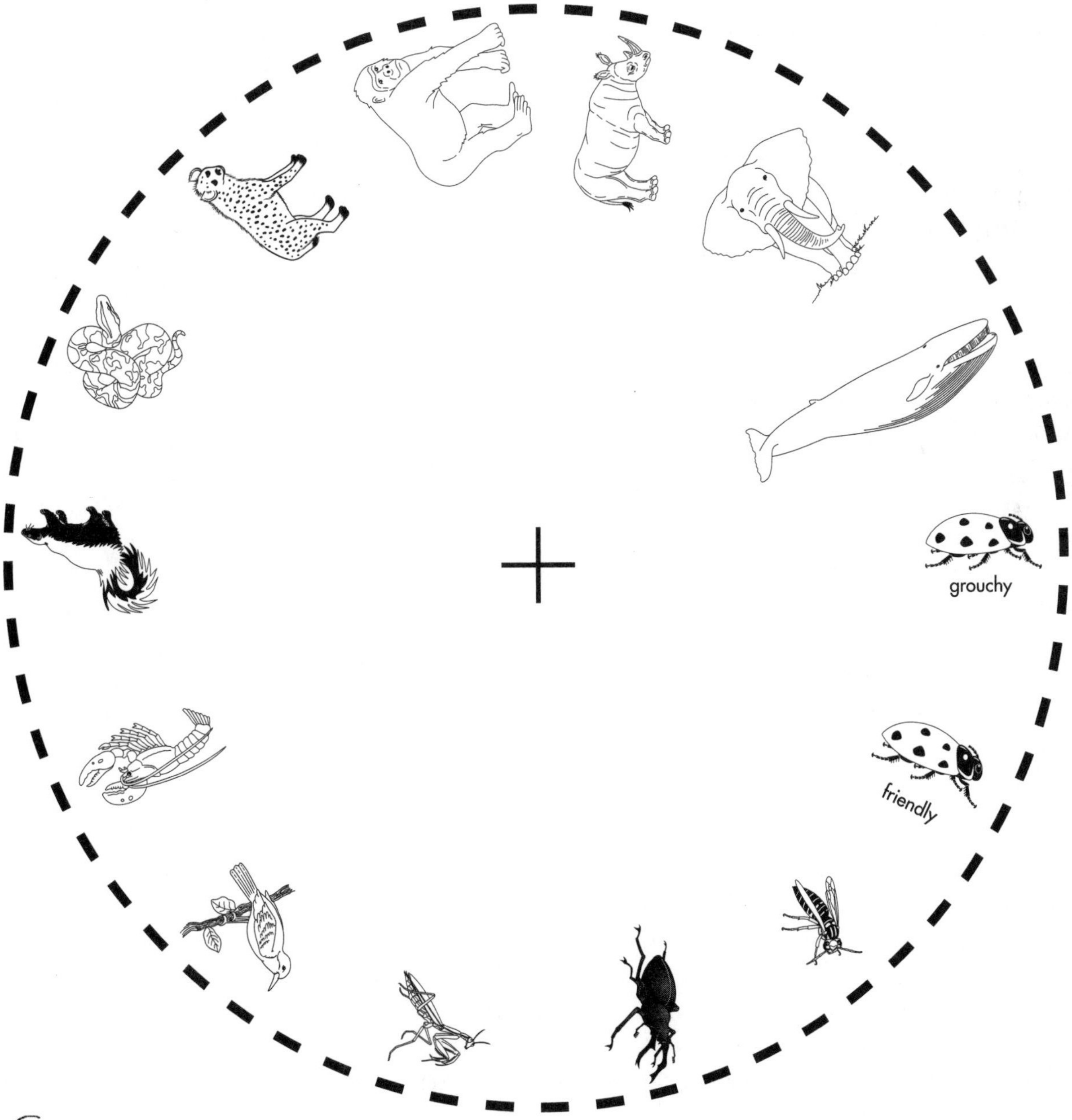

grouchy

friendly

Comprehension Activities

for *The Grouchy Ladybug*

Pre-reading Activity: Use the construction of this book to make predictions. Explain that a prediction is a guess about what might happen in a story. Inform students that when they read, they will find out if their predictions are correct. Draw a giant ladybug on the board. Make predictions as a class and record them on the ladybug. Draw a circle around each prediction, like a spot. Continue to preview the book. Point out the clocks at the tops of the pages. Ask students to look carefully at the clocks to see how many hours pass as the story unfolds. Then, ask them questions about how the different page sizes might relate to the sizes of the animals introduced in the story. Also, ask them to notice what happens to the print on each page. They should notice that the pages, print, and animals become larger and that hours are passing. Look at the illustrations with students and ask if they know where each type of animal lives. This will give them hints about where the ladybug flies during its adventure. Also, ask them to guess what the ladybug says to each animal based on the illustrations. (Don't let them read the print yet.) Ask students if they have other predictions to add to the ladybug drawing. After reading *The Grouchy Ladybug*, reread the predictions and color over the incorrect predictions to make spots.

During-reading Activity: Inform students that some stories take place over long periods of time. As you read the story to students, help them keep track of the time it takes for the ladybug to visit each animal during its adventure. Show students what five o'clock looks like on a teaching clock. Explain to students that you are starting at five o'clock because this is the time identified when the grouchy ladybug starts its adventure. Change the clock as you read the story. At the same time, put the word *hour* on the board. After one hour passes in the story, place a 1 before the word *hour*. After another hour passes in the story, explain to students that you must add an s to the word *hour* because the story is now taking more than one hour. Demonstrate by changing the 1 to a 2 and adding an s to *hour* to make *2 hours*. Continue until you get to the portion of the story that changes to increments of fifteen minutes. Explain that there are four fifteen-minute increments in one hour. At the end of the reading, help students understand that the story took 13 hours. Ask them why they think the ladybug is wet, tired, and hungry. To help them understand the concept of the time in the story better, have students relate time to their own lives. Ask students to tell you when they get up in the morning. Set the clock to this time and change the clock in increments of hours as students go through the things they do until they go to bed at night. Tally the hours as you did for the story.

Post-reading Activity: Discuss how the grouchy ladybug acted when it met the friendly ladybug. Ask, "Did the grouchy ladybug use good or bad manners when it spoke to each animal? Why? Was the ladybug using good sense when it asked the different animals to fight? Why or why not? How did the grouchy ladybug's attitude change when it wound up back in the same place after its travels? Why?" At the beginning of the story, the friendly ladybug was willing to share but the grouchy ladybug wasn't. Ask what lesson students think the grouchy ladybug learned 13 hours later. Have students write or dictate the answers to the questions on copies of the Comprehension Questions reproducible (page 57) so that you may assess their understanding of the story.

Comprehension Questions

comprehension reproducible for
The Grouchy Ladybug

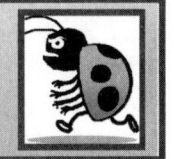

Name ______________________ Date ____________

Listen to your teacher read *The Grouchy Ladybug*. Write or dictate answers to the questions below.

1. How did the grouchy ladybug act when it met the friendly ladybug? ______________________

2. Did the grouchy ladybug use good or bad manners when it spoke to each animal? Why or why not? ______________________

3. Was it smart for the ladybug to ask the other animals to fight? Why or why not? ______________________

4. When the grouchy ladybug saw the friendly ladybug at the end of the story, how was the grouchy ladybug different? ______________________

5. What lesson did the grouchy ladybug learn? ______________________

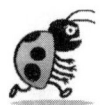

(G. P. Putnam's Sons, 1997)

Brett's beautifully written and illustrated book begins when the wind blows one of Little Lisa's socks off of the clothesline and it lands on a hedgehog's head. As various animals approach Hedgie to ask why he is wearing a hat, side panels provide illustrations to help readers predict events as the story unfolds. Hedgie has the last word as Lisa tries to gather her winter clothing from the inquisitive animals. This book can be used to teach foreshadowing, alliteration, contractions, questions, and word endings.

Related books: *Annie and the Wild Animals* by Jan Brett (Houghton Mifflin, 1989); *The Mitten* by Jan Brett (G. P. Putnam's Sons, 1989)

Phonemic Awareness Activities
for *The Hat*

Pre-reading Activity: Introduce the lesson to students by asking if they can tell you the two words in the title of the book as it appears on the cover. Ask them to listen for the sounds in each word as you slowly say them. Sing the song below to the tune of "If You're Happy and You Know It." After you sing the song and slowly say the sounds in the animal names (*hedgehog, pony,* etc.), have students identify the animals. Use this song to help students blend other words in the story as you read it aloud.

If you think you know the word, say the word.
If you think you know the word, say the word.
If you think you know the word
From the sounds that you have heard
If you think you know the word, say the word.
(Sound out a word for students to blend.)

During-reading Activity: Point out that Hedgie, a main character, has a name that begins with the /h/ sound. As you read the story aloud, ask students to listen for words that begin with the /h/ sound, like *hat*. When they hear a word, have them clap and repeat it. Have them sound out each word that begins with h.

Post-reading Activity: Cut out the picture cards on the We All Wear the Hat reproducible (page 59). Place them in a hat. Have students take turns choosing picture cards from the hat. Have each student say her picture name and its initial sound, then name something else with the same initial sound. Repeat this activity, but have students select cards, then listen for and repeat the ending sounds.

We All Wear the Hat

phonemic awareness reproducible for
The Hat

Name_____ Date _____

Cut out the pictures and place them in a hat. Have each student select a card, say the name of the picture, identify the initial sound of the word, and name another word with the same initial sound. Play the game again to identify ending sounds.

Phonics Activities
for *The Hat*

Pre-reading Activity: Point out the word *hat* in the book title. Explain to students that the word *hat* is part of a family of words containing the /at/ sound. Use the alphabet cards (pages 159-160) to place the word *hat* in a pocket chart. Ask students to replace the h with a card containing the letter b. Demonstrate how to blend the /b/ sound with the /at/ sound. Continue this exercise by using other consonants to create new at family words. Have students cut out triangles and small circles from construction paper, then glue the circles to the tops of the triangles (like pom-poms) to create their own winter hats. Instruct each student to write *at* on the circle and to list words in the at family on the triangles. Attach a piece of string to a bulletin board like a clothesline and use clothespins to fasten the hats to the string. Title the bulletin board "Hats Off to the AT Family."

During-reading Activity: Explain to students that they will be going on a Blend Search. There are many words in the story that begin with *consonant blends*—two consonants that appear together in a word, with each retaining its sound when blended. Write the following blends on index cards: *tr, dr, cl, st, fl, fr, sn, br, bl.* Show each card to students and ask them to think of words that begin with each blend. After this review, place the cards in a hat. Pair students and have each pair select a card from the hat. Explain that it is their job to search for words in the story that contain the blend on the card. Provide multiple copies of *The Hat*. As students read the book and find words, instruct them to write the words on the cards under the blend. Have them continue until they have listed all of the words they can find. Instruct them to work together to identify each word. Remind them to use the blend and the final sound to try to pronounce each word. Review the words found and create a class chart for each of the blends explored. Ask students if they can offer other words that begin with blends that are not in the book.

Post-reading Activity: Use the Blend Bingo reproducible (page 61) to reinforce the recognition of initial consonant blends (consonant clusters) and words in the story. Explain to each student that on her game board, she should write the twenty words listed on the reproducible. She can write them in any order, but instruct her not to use words more than once. Then, as you call out the words, have students use paper scraps or pennies to cover the words they hear. When a student covers a full vertical row, she can call out "Blend bingo!" In order to win, she must be able to say the words in her covered row and identify the initial blends. Reward winners with prizes that contain blends such as silly straws, animal crackers, pretzels, stickers, crayons, extra free time, etc. Challenge winners to identify the blends in their prizes.

Name_____ Date _____

Write one of these words in each square: clothes, stuck, clucked, flipped, from, stockings, snowstorm, brambles, blows, snorted, startled, tree, dry, straw, friendly, clothesline, snowy, started, prickles, blew. Then, play Blend Bingo.

Blend Bingo

Vocabulary Activities
for *The Hat*

Pre-reading Activity: Point out to students that there are many words that are used frequently in stories and that if they memorize these words and learn to recognize them by sight, they will become better readers. There are approximately 47 words in *The Hat* that are considered high-frequency. Refer to the Frequently Used Words reproducible (page 63) for a list of these words. Write each word on an index card and show the cards to students. Display large letters across a bulletin board. Attach each word under its beginning letter on the bulletin board to make a word wall. To make the board interactive, use felt to line the bulletin board and attach hook-and-loop tape to the backs of the cards. Allow students to say and read the words, sort the cards, alphabetize them, remove them and spell the words from memory, etc.

During-reading Activity: Point out just before reading the story that some words have been shortened by using *apostrophes* and that these words are called *contractions*. Explain that an apostrophe is also used to show ownership or possession. There are two places in the story where the apostrophe shows ownership. In all other cases, the apostrophes are used to make contractions. Write the following words on a piece of chart paper and ask students to read them: *what is, it is, is not, I will, did not, do not, that is, does not, would not*. Have multiple copies of *The Hat* available. Ask groups to look for different words with apostrophes as they read the story. As each group finds its contractions, have them write each one on an index card and tape the card under the two words on the chart paper that they think the contraction represents. When all of the contractions are identified, stop the search and talk about students' matches and the letters that are replaced by the apostrophes. (Tell them to ignore *Hedgie's head* and *dog's ears* since the apostrophes in these instances show ownership.) Ask students if they can think of other contractions to add to the chart. Keep the chart posted and challenge students to add to the contraction list as they read other books.

Post-reading Activity: Explain to students that there are many action words or verbs in the text of the story that end in ed or ing. Challenge groups of students to search for these words. Have them create a chart to list the words under the headings *ed* and *ing*. To make sure the words are truly action words, ask students to play a game of charades to act out the action each word implies. As students guess the action for a word, add a check next to it on the chart. Students should discover the following action words in the story: *hanging, watching, looking, laughing, running, thinking, chasing, poked, pulled, clucked, laughed, cocked, flipped, tugged, barked, wanted, purred, carried, wearing, headed, yelped, giggled, perked, squealed, asked, snorted, shouted, looked, called, started*. They will discover that *stocking* is not used here as a verb and that some words are adjectives such as *embarrassing, missing, startled, tired*, etc.

Name_____ Date _____

Refer to these high-frequency words as you read, *The Hat.* Add other high-frequency words as you read other books.

a: a, all, an, and, are, as

b: back, be, but, by

c: called

d: down

f: for

h: had, has, he, her, his, how

i: I, if, in, is, it

l: look

m: me, my

n: no

o: of, off, on

s: said, she, so

t: that, the, them, they, this, to

u: up

w: was, what, when, will, with

y: you

Fluency Activities
for *The Hat*

Pre-reading Activity: Talk about the sounds that animals make. Provide pictures of animals and ask students to think of what sounds each animal might make. Let students compare their answers with the sounds identified in the book. Name the animals from the book and ask students to mimic the sounds as they think the animals may make them. Extend the activity by having students make other animal noises. Play a guessing game to let students guess which animal noises their classmates are making.

During-reading Activity: As you read the story for a first time, point out the quotation marks. Remind students that quotation marks are usually used to show that something is being said. Have them reread the story, but this time assign students different parts. Inform them that when their characters are mentioned by the narrator (a student), they will be expected to read the quoted statements or questions of the animals or Lisa. Before reading, practice different types of sentences: statements, questions, exclamations, and commands. Remind students to think about how their quotes should be read. Record the reading and play it back for students. Ask them to evaluate how well they read their parts and think of ways to improve their oral reading. After a period of practice, have them reread their parts again while being recorded. Ask them to compare recordings to determine if they read better the second time.

Post-reading Activity: After working with students on reading *The Hat* aloud, use the Rate My Reading reproducible (page 65) to evaluate fluency. Have another teacher or a parent volunteer listen to students read designated text from *The Hat*. Remind the volunteer to put each student's name on the reproducible. As the volunteer listens to each student, have her fill out information about the student's reading. (Listen to a few students read to spot-check the accuracy of the evaluations.) Collect the reproducibles and review them. Use the results to decide which students need extra help with fluency. If students work with reading partners, assign strong readers to read aloud with struggling ones.

Rate My Reading
fluency reproducible for
The Hat

Name_____   Date _____

Listen to the student read from *The Hat.* Circle the responses below that best describe how fluently the student reads.

The student's voice was loud and clear.   yes no somewhat

The student knew most words.   yes no

The student sounded natural, just
as if he/she were talking normally.   yes no somewhat

The student was expressive.   yes no somewhat

The student paused at punctuation.   yes no somewhat

The student did not repeat anything.   yes no

Comments: _____

_____

_____

_____

_____

_____

_____

Comprehension Activities
for *The Hat*

re-reading Activity: Discuss the title *The Hat*, and the illustrations on the front and back covers of the book. Students can learn many things about the characters, time, and setting, and can possibly predict the problems and solutions by looking at the cover illustrations. Cut a large sheet of bulletin board paper and hang it on the board horizontally. Title it "The Hat-Making Predictions" and write the following headings across the top to create four separate columns: *characters*, *time and setting*, *problems*, and *solutions*. Based on what students see on the book cover, ask them to predict who is part of the story, when and where it takes place, and what problems and solutions may occur. As they offer suggestions, write them in the appropriate columns. Cut a piece of paper to resemble a picture frame to cover the side panels in the book. Look through the book with students, showing them the main illustration in the center of each two-page spread. Ask students if they would like to change or add to their predictions based on what they see in the illustrations. Alter the predictions accordingly and check them after reading.

uring-reading Activity: As you read the story with students, point out the picture frames at the sides of each main illustration. Ask students to describe the picture in each frame. After a few pages, students should realize that some of the pictures are used to foreshadow what is coming next in the story, while other frames tell a different story about what Lisa is doing as Hedgie is being questioned by each of the animals. Have students use the frames they think tell Lisa's story to predict the events in the main story. Have them notice that as the story unfolds, some of the animals in the frames pick up articles of clothing. Before you read the last two pages, ask students what they think the animals do with the clothing. Have each student use a copy of the Blank Book reproducible (page 67) to add one more prediction to continue the story. Ask him to draw something that would give clues about how the story continues.

ost-reading Activity: Refer back to the picture frames from the during-reading activity and ask students to find the ones that tell Lisa's story. Explain that these frames tell a story within a story. While Hedgie was being questioned by all of the animals, Lisa was busy doing chores and other things. Have students work in pairs to draw and write sentences in chronological order about all of the things that Lisa did. Put the pictures together in a class book. Refer back to the pre-reading prediction chart and ask students to evaluate their assumptions about the story. Why couldn't they predict that Lisa was doing things as Hedgie's story was unfolding? Were they able to identify the problems and the solutions? Now that they have seen the other animals wearing the clothing, could they think of another problem in the story?

First-Rate Reading™ Grade 1 • CD-0069 • © Carson-Dellosa

Name_____ Date _____

Use the blank book frame below to draw a picture that will give hints about what might happen at the end of the story, *The Hat.*

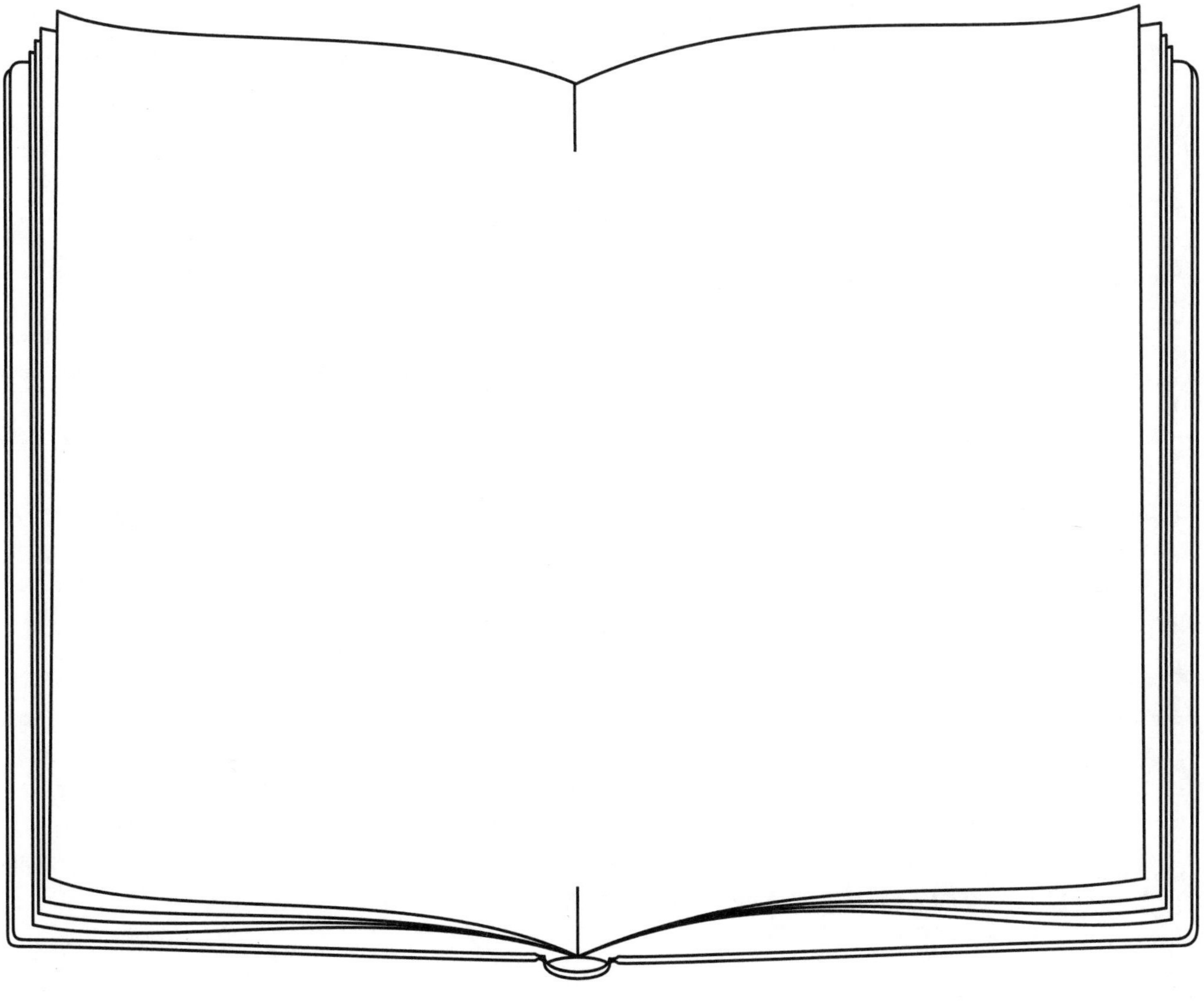

(Laura Geringer, 2002)

If You Take a Mouse to School tells about a boy who takes a mouse to school in a lunch box. The text is simple, but the illustrations relate funny details. Use the book to teach sequencing and compound words.

Related books: *If You Give a Moose a Muffin* by Laura Joffe Numeroff (HarperCollins Juvenile Books, 1991); *If You Give a Mouse a Cookie* by Laura Joffe Numeroff (HarperCollins Juvenile Books, 2000)

Phonemic Awareness Activities
for *If You Take a Mouse to School*

Pre-reading Activity: Have each student draw a mouse, cut it out, and tape a craft stick to the back to make a puppet. Cut out and distribute the picture cards on the What Do I Need for School? reproducible (page 69). Explain that in this story a mouse packs food and supplies in a lunch box to bring to school. Provide a lunch box. Have students help the mouse pack the lunch box by listening to the key words and sounds of items packed by the mouse. If the initial sound on the card matches the initial sound of the item the mouse packed, have a student place the card in the lunch box. For example, have the mouse puppet say, "I have a lunch box, and I want some *bananas* to go in it." Exaggerate the /b/ sound. The student with a picture of books should raise his card and say the word *books*. Have the mouse "repeat" the words *bananas* and *books*. Exaggerate the /b/ sound as you say the words. Then, let the class repeat. Continue until all cards are in the lunch box. (Note that this author spells *lunch box* as a compound word: *lunchbox*.)

During-reading Activity: Ask students to listen carefully as you say the word *mouse*, and have them identify the sound they hear at the end of the word (/s/). Say a set of three words such as *pets*, *cats*, and *dog*. Ask students to identify the two words in each list that end with the /s/ sound. As you read the story, have them listen for words that end with the /s/ sound. When you come to a word that ends with the /s/ sound, remind them to say /s/. Read the story slowly so that they can hear the word endings but not so slowly as to sound unnatural. They should be able to recognize the /s/ sound at the end of *mouse*, *house*, *blocks*, *stops*, *science*, *nice*, *place*, *books*, *bus*, and *baskets*. Note that *things*, *rings*, *pencils*, *chances*, *use*, and *he's* end with /z/, and *lunchbox* ends in x (/ks/).

Post-reading Activity: The main setting of the story is a school. Have students say *school*, then take off the /sk/ sound and say the ool. Ask them to think of other words that end with ool like *cool*, *fool*, and *pool*. Then, have students say *goof*, *roof*, and *spoon*. Ask if they can hear the difference. Explain that when a vowel is followed by the letter l, the sound changes because it is l-controlled. Read a list of words in random order such as *drool*, *spool*, *tool*, *moon*, *soon*, *loot*, *root*, and *zoom*. When students hear the l-controlled /oo/ sound, have them raise their hands and repeat the word. Adjust the lesson for any regional dialect differences, particularly *root* and *roof*.

What Do I Need for School?
phonemic awareness reproducible for
If You Take a Mouse to School

Name_____ Date _____

Cut out the pictures and distribute them to students to play the initial sound game in the phonemic awareness pre-reading activity.

Phonics Activities
for *If You Take a Mouse to School*

Pre-reading Activity: Explain that the word *mouse* has a special vowel sound. The /ow/ sound is called a *diphthong*. Tell students that they can also hear this sound in the words *house* and *cow*. Create two columns, one for words containing ou and one for words containing ow. Have students suggest other words with the /ow/ sound. List them in the appropriate columns. Have students draw mice on construction paper and cut them out. Have each student write one ou or ow word on each mouse. Collect the mice. After students leave for the day, hide the mice around the room. Divide a bulletin board in half. Label one side of the board ow and the other side ou. Allow students time to search for mice and attach them to the bulletin board on the appropriate sides. Inform students that they may find other words containing the letters ou or ow as they read *If You Take a Mouse To School*. Let students add mice as they discover the words.

During-reading Activity: Introduce the consonant digraphs sh and ch by giving examples of words that contain each. Explain that these digraphs can be the beginnings, middles, or ends of words, like *sheep* and *fish*, *hatched* and *wishing*, or *chop* and *catch*. As you read the story, have students say /sh/ or /ch/ when they spot a story word containing either digraph. Ask them to identify whether the sound is in an initial, medial, or final position. Write the words found on two separate charts. Write the digraphs in a different color from the rest of the letters in the words so that students can see at a glance if the sound is an initial or final one. Some of the words students will find include *lunchbox*, *sandwich*, *share*, *wash*, *lunch*, *bookshelf*, *finished*, *shoot*, *catch*, and *chances*. Note that *school* is an exception because the ch makes the /k/ sound. Also, note that *lunchbox* is usually spelled as two words, but the author spells it as one in this book.

Post-reading Activity: Provide multiple copies of the book for this activity. Explain to students that they can use consonants as clues to figure out vowels and read entire words. Give them a few words with missing vowels. For example, *sh_p* can be either *ship* or *shop*. *M__se* can be *mouse* or *moose*. Give students the *M_ss_ng V_w_ls* reproducible (page 71) and ask them to work in pairs to figure out the vowels that are missing in the words listed. Inform them that the words are located somewhere in the story. Ask them to search the story to verify that their guesses are correct.

M_ss_ng V_w_ls
phonics reproducible for
If You Take a Mouse to School

Name_____ Date _____

Fill in the missing vowels in each word. Then, search for the words in the book to make sure your vowels are correct.

m _ _ se

l _ nchb _ x

n _ t _ b _ _ k

b _ ckp _ ck

w _ sh

bl _ cks

b _ _ ks

t _ ck

st _ ps

sch _ _ l

sn _ ck

p _ nc _ ls

m _ th

l _ nchr _ _ m

h _ _ se

h _ m _

sh _ _ t

b _ ck

Vocabulary Activities
for *If You Take a Mouse to School*

Pre-reading Activity: There are some hard words in the story, but explain to students that they can learn these words by associating them with pictures or other words that they know. Write the words on index cards as words that the mouse should learn along with them. Tape them to the board, leaving space between them so that you can write a definition under each card. Say the words *probably, experiment, furniture, cafeteria,* and *breath*. Ask volunteers to say what each word means. If they have trouble with a word, use it in a sentence. Encourage them to think of easier words that mean the same thing; for example, *probably* means maybe or almost sure, *experiment* means to try a new thing, etc. Write their definitions under the vocabulary words. As you read the story, ask students to refer to the board as they hear each word read to make sure they know its meaning in the story.

During-reading Activity: Explain to students that they will hear compound words in the story. Remind them that a *compound word* is made up of two smaller words that, when separated, can stand alone with their own meanings. Ask students to give some examples. As they read the story, have them find the seven compound words (*lunchbox, notebook, backpack, bathroom, lunchroom, bookshelf, skateboarding*). Note that *lunchbox* is usually spelled as two words, but the author uses it as one in this book. Write the words on the board or on a piece of chart paper as students find them. After reading the story, give students blank pieces of paper. Ask each student to fold the paper in thirds by folding the ends so that they meet in the middle of the paper, making two creases. (Once unfolded, the center column will be twice as wide as the left or right column.) In the middle column, have each student copy a compound word from the list. Then, ask him to fold both ends of the paper over so that the compound word can't be seen. Next, have him write the first half of the compound on the left flap and the second half of the word on the right flap. Have him repeat this process for each word. These cards will help students see which two words make up each compound word. Have students use the cards to practice saying the words. Challenge them to create more fold-over cards for other compound words.

Post-reading Activity: Explain to students that in the story the author used words that sound the same but are spelled differently and have different meanings. Inform them that these types of words are called *homophones*. Help students search the text to find the words *to, too,* and *two* and read the sentence that contains each word. From the sentences they should be able to determine what each word means. Inform them that the author used other words in the story that are homophones. Have them find the words *read, for, do, see, some, one, so,* and *in*. Ask them to read the sentence that contains each word to understand its meaning. Can they think of other words that sound the same as but have different meanings than the words that they found in the text? Use the Hunting for Homophones reproducible (page 73) to challenge students to use the correct homophone to complete each sentence.

Hunting for Homophones
vocabulary reproducible for
If You Take a Mouse to School

Name_____   Date _____

Use the following homophones to fill in the sentences correctly: see, sea; won, one; write, right; to, two, too; sum, some; for, four.

I use a pen to _____ .

I love when my teacher says I'm _____ .

The _____ of three plus three is six.

_____ of us can add.

I _____ the spelling bee.

I was the only _____ to win.

Two plus two is _____ .

I have a gift _____ you.

The mouse can _____ you.

The boat is at _____ .

The mouse went _____ school.

I want to go, _____ .

_____ of us will go.

Fluency Activities
for *If You Take a Mouse to School*

Pre-reading Activity: Use this exercise to emphasize how reading to an audience elicits reactions. Explain that students will be reading a story about a mouse who goes to school. Ask them to pretend they will have a mouse "student" visiting their classroom, and that they need to provide him with a list of classroom rules so that he will know what to do and what not to do. Give copies of the Classroom Rules reproducible (page 75) to students. Instruct them to pretend that they are in charge of giving the new mouse the official "Rules for New Students" presentation. Let each student write a short list of rules and practice reading the list several times. Then, pretend to be the mouse, because students will enjoy reading you the rules! (Or, have a student or other volunteer be the mouse.) Have a student read her list to the "mouse." If you are the mouse, react appropriately but do not interrupt. Choose another student to read his rules. Depending on the tone in the next student's voice, and on the rules themselves, react differently. Ask students what differences they notice in the rules and in the reactions, and why they think the "mouse" reacted differently. Point out that if students were less fluent when reading the rules, you may have reacted differently or misunderstood. Finally, compare the rules with what the mouse in the book actually does when he gets to school.

During-reading Activity: Read *If You Take a Mouse to School* as a class, then assign students to four groups. Provide a copy of the book for each group. Divide the pages so that the first group practices the text about the mouse at home, the second group reads text about the mouse at school, the third group reads text about the mouse building his house and reading books, and the fourth group reads about the mouse as he leaves school. Have the groups chorally read their assigned parts. Remind them to watch for punctuation marks that will tell them when to pause. Point out a dash and an exclamation point, and explain how to pause and use proper tone with these punctuation marks. When students are ready, have groups gather to read the different parts of the book with you.

Post-reading Activity: Explain to students that a good method of learning to read with fluency is to practice something called *alliteration*. On the board, write the sentence *Mouse made many math mistakes.* and ask students to help you read it. After they read the sentence, ask them to tell you what they notice about the sentence. They will realize that each word begins with the same letter and sound. Inform them that when consecutive words in a sentence begin with the same sound, this is called *alliteration*. Give them the following sentences to practice: *Please pass paper and pencils; Mouse must make many messes; Blue backpacks belong on buses;* and *School science seems super.* Give students time to say the sentences a few times slowly and then ask them to practice saying each sentence quickly three times.

Classroom Rules
fluency reproducible for
If You Take a Mouse to School

Name _____ Date _____

A mouse student is joining your class! On the lines below, write a short list of classroom rules the mouse should follow. Practice reading them at least five times.

Rule #1: _____

_____

_____

_____

Rule #2: _____

_____

_____

_____

Rule #3: _____

_____

_____

_____

Rule #4: _____

_____

_____

_____

Comprehension Activities
for *If You Take a Mouse to School*

Pre-reading Activity: Prior to reading the title, draw attention to the cover illustration. Ask students what clues in the illustration indicate that the story will be fictional. (There's a mouse wearing overalls and holding a pencil while sitting on a lunch box.) Have students think about the title of the story and what it implies. If you take a mouse to school, what will happen? How will he get there? What will he bring with him? Inform students that the mouse travels to school in a boy's lunch box and he brings some things with him. Have each student create a lunch box by decorating a shoe box that she brings from home. After students decorate their "lunch boxes," have them fill the lunch boxes with pictures of things they think a mouse will bring with him and will need on his first day of school. Ask students to draw pictures or write sentences that give predictions about what the mouse will do in school. Remind them to relate the mouse's activities to what they needed to get ready for their first day of school and what they did when they got there. Also, ask each student to write a note to the mouse to make him feel welcome at school and place it in her lunch box. Have students close their lunch boxes and put them aside. After reading the story, invite them to determine if their predictions were correct.

During-reading Activity: Read the story with students and discuss all of the things the mouse did to get ready for school, then have them point out all of the things the mouse did during school. Lastly, have them talk about what the mouse did to prepare to leave school. Create story webs with students. Have students write *A Mouse's Day at School* in the center circle and title other circles *Getting Ready*, *At School*, *Leaving School*, and *The Next Day*. Have students fill in the first three outer circles in the web with the information they learned from the book. In the last circle, ask students to write what they think might happen if the mouse returns to school the next day. Ask them to use the webs to summarize the facts in the story and predict new endings by extending the story. Some students may need to use pictures to retell parts of the story. Allow them to use sentences, pictures, or both.

Post-reading Activity: Look through the items students put in their lunch boxes during the pre-reading activity. Ask them to determine if their predictions were correct. Talk about the things that the mouse did in school. Ask each student to relate one special "mouse moment" by describing what she thinks the mouse had the most fun doing. Inform students that the author of this book has also written similar books such as *If You Give a Mouse a Cookie* and *If You Give a Moose a Muffin* (see related books, page 68). Point out that each of these stories is a circular story because the character always ends where he started. (In this book, the mouse left home to go to school only to return at the end of the day.) Ask students to use the graphic organizer on the Circular Stories reproducible (page 77) to take notes about their own circular stories about a kitten. Ask them to think of things a kitten can do or where she can go and fill in the different sections, making sure that the stories end where they began. Help students brainstorm a list of things they know about kittens to get them started. Include favorite foods, toys, places to visit, things kittens do, and other animals they like to play with or chase. Let students write or dictate the stories on additional sheets of paper.

Name _____ Date _____

Use the graphic organizer to write notes about a short, circular story about a kitten. Then, write the story on another sheet of paper.

_____

_____

_____

_____

_____

_____   _____

_____   _____

_____   _____

_____   _____

_____   _____

_____

_____

_____

_____

 _____

Is Your Mama a Llama?
by Deborah Guarino
(Scholastic, 1991)

This delightful rhyming tale is about a baby llama who asks all of his friends if their mamas are llamas. It will engage young readers with its factual text and realistic illustrations. Use this book to teach rhyming words, synonyms, types of sentences, and foreshadowing.

Related books: *Have You Seen My Cat?* by Eric Carle (Simon & Schuster, 1991); *If My Mom Were a Platypus* by Dia L. Michels (Platypus Media, 2001); *Where Is My Baby?* by Harriet Ziefert (Handprint Books, 2002)

Phonemic Awareness Activities
for *Is Your Mama a Llama?*

Pre-reading Activity: Say the words *mama* and *llama*. Ask students how these two words are alike. (They rhyme.) Ask students if they know any other words that rhyme. Play a game in which you say three words and students identify the word that does not rhyme. Say, "Dave, go, gave; cave, cook, behave; Fred, ran, said; wings, things, wet; say, Jane, explain; do, moo, bark; replied, clam, Clyde; day, night, way; me, mom, be; Llyn, smile, grin; hair, her, fur; toy, too, you; friend, dad, end." Challenge each student to think of three words (two that rhyme and one that doesn't) to say to the class.

During-reading Activity: Point out the animal pictures on the book cover. Copy and distribute the Animal Rhyme Time reproducible (page 79), and have students color and cut out the animals. Ask students to say the animals' names. Borrow one of each animal from students and line them up on the board. Tell students that as you read the story, they should listen for rhyming words. Before you turn a page to reveal each animal, repeat the word in the text that rhymes with the animal and ask a volunteer to find that rhyming animal on the board. Have the student repeat the two rhyming words and then have the class repeat them. When you have finished the story, have students look at their animal pictures and try to think of additional words that rhyme with them. Save these picture cards for the pre-reading phonics activity.

Post-reading Activity: Brainstorm a list of additional animals on the board. Help students think of short animal names that belong to common word families such as *cat*, *dog*, *pig*, etc. Let each student choose an animal and think of a word that rhymes with the animal. Then, allow pairs to work together to write new animal riddles in the style of *Is Your Mama a Llama?* Help students with relevant animal facts and rhyming structure. When students are finished, let them present their riddles to the class.

Animal Rhyme Time

phonemic awareness reproducible for
Is Your Mama a Llama?

Name _____   Date _____

Color and cut out the animals on this page. Your teacher will tell you how to use them for a rhyming activity.

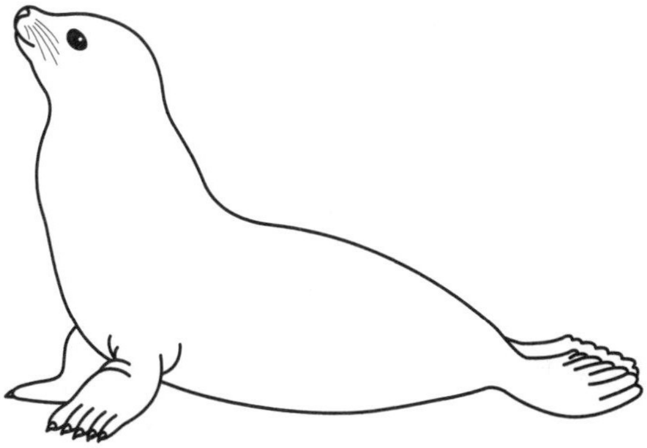

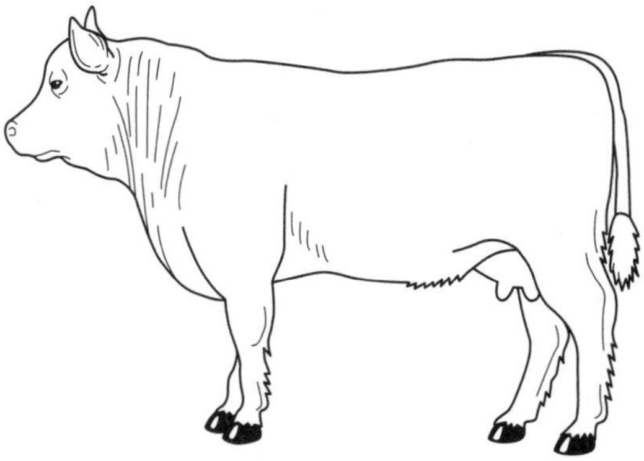

Phonics Activities
for *Is Your Mama a Llama?*

Pre-reading Activity: Use the animal picture cards from the Animal Rhyme Time reproducible (page 79) in this activity. Instruct students to name each animal as you hold up a card. Then, ask students to name the sound of the first letter of the word, then the ending sound, then any vowels. Write the correct spelling on the board and attach each card beside its spelling. Continue until all of the animals' names are spelled correctly. Give students construction paper, glue, and chenille craft sticks or cooked, cooled spaghetti. Have each student choose one animal from the board and "spell" its name by bending the chenille craft sticks or spaghetti into the shapes of the letters in the word. Let students glue the letters to construction paper. When students are finished, have them draw pictures of their animals on white construction paper and attach their words to the bottoms. Have them share their work and practice sounding out the words and making the animal noises for fun.

During-reading Activity: Explain to students that one of the mothers in the story can lay eggs. Ask if they know which one (the swan). Pretend the swan laid 12 eggs. On 12 plastic eggs, write the following word endings: *ave, ings, ite, at, on, ay, er, eel, ow, end, ane,* and *e*. Display the eggs in an open egg carton. Hold up each egg one at a time and repeat the sound. Tell students that as you read the story you want them to listen for words that rhyme with the ending sounds on the eggs. Read the story, and pause each time a student thinks she can rhyme a word from the story to an ending sound on an egg. Have her say the word she thinks rhymes and then walk over and pick up the egg the word rhymes with. Have the rest of the class put their thumbs up if they think the words rhyme and their thumbs down if they don't. Write each rhyming word on a yellow circle to represent a yolk and have the student put it in the correct egg. Continue until the book is finished. Challenge students to think of other words that rhyme with the endings on the eggs. Write them on yellow circles and add them to the eggs. Close the eggs and place them in a center for individual practice.

Post-reading Activity: Tell students that they are going to play a game with letters. Hand out the Letter Toss reproducible (page 81), and have students lightly color and then cut out each letter square. (Each student will need to make one extra a and w card.) Write the words *bat, kangaroo, swan, seal, llama,* and *cow* on the board. Tell students you are going say one of the words from the board, and that when you say "Go," they should throw their letters up in the air (not too high) and try to find the letters to spell that word as quickly as possible. Then, have students spell all of the words while they are listed on the board. Finally, have students try to spell the words by sounding them out after they have been erased from the board. Have students spell and decode the words by listening for the beginning and ending sounds, and then for the vowels. Have students use the letter cards later to create their own simple words. Allow them to practice sounding out and writing the words that they make.

Letter Toss

phonics reproducible for
Is Your Mama a Llama?

Name _____ Date _____

Color and cut out each letter. On a sheet of paper, make extra letter a and w cards and cut them out. Listen for instructions from your teacher.

a	a	a	a	a
a	b	c	e	g
k	l	l	l	m
n	n	o	o	o
r	s	s	t	w

Vocabulary Activities
for *Is Your Mama a Llama?*

Pre-reading Activity: Write the following vocabulary words on a piece of chart paper: *answered, asked, explained, replied,* and *responded.* Ask students if they know any of the words on the chart. After students have volunteered their answers, read the words aloud. Tell students that when authors want to make their writing more interesting, they try to use different words in their stories. In this story, the author uses all of these words instead of *said.* Model how each word might be used in place of *said.* Distribute copies of the Don't Say Said! reproducible (page 83). Have students fill in the blank in each sentence with a word from the word bank. When students are finished, call on volunteers to read their sentences. Challenge students to make up their own sentences using these new vocabulary words.

During-reading Activity: Ask students if they remember the words from the pre-reading activity that the author uses in place of *said.* Show them the list of vocabulary words. Explain that as you read the story you would like them to say, "Stop!" every time they hear one of those words. When students say, "Stop!" pause and read the sentence again. Ask students if they think any of the other vocabulary words could be used in place of the present one. When you have finished reading the story, go back to the sentences that have *said* in them. Reread these sentences one at a time and challenge students to replace *said* with one of the vocabulary words from the list.

Post-reading Activity: Prior to this activity, write sentences from the story on sentence strips. Make a second set of the same sentences, then cut these into individual words. Put the sentence strips in a pocket chart in scrambled order. Ask students to help you read the sentences and put them in the correct story order. They may need to refer to the story for help. Once the sentences are in order, tell students that you have the same sentences cut into pieces and you need their help to put them back together. Display the word cards and ask "Is there anyone who can find the first word for me?" When a student finds a word, have her place it on top of the word on the sentence strip and pronounce the word for the class. Continue until each sentence is complete and then have the class read the sentences chorally to practice the words and retell the story. Once students complete this activity a few times, make a new set of cards using synonyms for some of the story words. Post the uncut sentence strips again and let students take turns replacing some of the sentence words with their synonyms. Store the activity in a center along with extra blank cards so that students can think of and create cards for their own synonyms.

Name_____ Date _____

Use a word in the word bank to complete each sentence. You can use a word more than once.

Word bank: answered, explained, replied, responded, asked

1. "Where is my bunny?" _____ Ricky.

2. "I saw her under your bed," _____ Diana.

3. "Oh, no, that is not good!" _____ Ricky.

4. "She was only resting," _____ Diana.

5. "But you don't understand. The last time she was under my bed, she had baby bunnies!" _____ Ricky.

6. "Can we go see?"
   _____ Diana.

7. "Yes, and we should hurry!"
   _____ Ricky.

Fluency Activities
for *Is Your Mama a Llama?*

Pre-reading Activity: Tell students that in *Is Your Mama a Llama?* they will hear many questions. Ask students which punctuation mark comes at the end of a question. Draw a large question mark on the board. Tell students that when they ask questions they raise their voices slightly at the ends of the sentences. Model for students how to ask a question. Have students practice this by asking each other questions. Then, read some of the questions from the story so that students are prepared to identify them during the reading.

During-reading Activity: Prior to this activity, gather a blank tape and a tape recorder. Tell students that they will hear the baby llama ask many questions in this story. Tell them to listen carefully to your voice as you read. Have each student form a question mark with his hands (hold the right hand cupped like a c and the index finger on the left hand under the right hand when he hears a question). Have the class repeat each question together. When the story is finished, allow students to hear themselves ask questions. Record each student as he asks a question. Play it back and ask the student if he used the right voice for the question. If the answer is no, allow him to try again. For additional practice, record one student asking a question and another student answering it. Ask students to explain how their voices differed.

Post-reading Activity: Prior to this activity, make large punctuation marks out of black construction paper (two periods, one exclamation point, and one question mark). Tape the parts of the exclamation point and question mark together. Draw a period, an exclamation point, and a question mark on the board or on a piece of chart paper. Ask students what these marks are used for and when they would use one. Write a statement, an exclamatory sentence, a command, and a question on the board. Also, write each type of sentence on the board and draw the proper punctuation marks next to it. Have students sit in a circle. Place the large, paper punctuation marks in the center of the circle on the floor. Tell students that you will say a sentence and if they know which punctuation mark goes at the end, they should raise their hands. As you call on a student, have her go to the center of the circle, pick up the correct ending punctuation mark, and then think of a similar sentence to tell the class. Remind students to use the correct intonation when saying their sentences. Continue until each student has had a turn. Have students return to their seats, then distribute the .?! reproducible (page 85) so that they can practice saying sentences correctly to each other.

Name_____ Date _____

Work in pairs to choose the correct punctuation mark for the end of each sentence. (Look at the marks on the right side of this page for help.) Then, practice reading the sentences together with the correct tone.

Jane has a new bike__

How many dogs are playing__

Do your work__

The house is on fire__

It's my birthday__

Joey fell down and cut his knee__

Who broke the dish__

My cat is sleeping__

Close the door__

.

?

!

Comprehension Activities

for *Is Your Mama a Llama?*

**P**re-reading Activity: Show students the cover of the book. Read the title to them. Ask students who might be asking the question, "Is your mama a llama?" Explain that in this story, the baby llama asks everyone if their mamas are llamas. Discuss animals and their babies. Ask students if they know the name of a baby bat (pup), a baby bear (cub), a baby swan (cygnet), a baby cow (calf), a baby seal (pup), a baby horse (foal), a baby duck (duckling), a baby kangaroo (joey), and a baby llama (cria). Talk about other animals and their babies. Create a chart identifying animals and babies in the story. Add any other pairs that the class suggests. Finally, give students copies of the Baby Animals reproducible (page 87). Have students match the mother animals to their babies.

During-reading Activity: Explain to students that this book is fun to read because the author gives clues about each animal. Students can guess each animal before turning a page. Share with students that this writing technique is called *foreshadowing*. The author also made this a rhyming book, so if students listen closely to each clue and think of an animal that rhymes with the last word in the clue, they will be able to name the animal. Read the story aloud, pausing before each animal is named so that students have time to think about the clue and what animal name will fit with the rhyme. When you think they are ready, reread the last two sentences and have them shout out the animal name as you turn the page. At the end of the story, ask students to remember the clues the author gave for specific animals. Give students clues about other animals they should be able to name. Challenge them to give clues to their classmates about animals they know. Next, play a game similar to musical chairs. Place chairs in a circle (one chair per student). Place a picture of an animal mother on each chair back. Let each student march around the chairs, and when the music stops, find a chair to sit on. When students sit, read them a rhyme from the story about an animal mother (or a rhyme that you have made up for the other animal pictures on the chairs) but leave out the animal's name. If a student is sitting on a chair with a picture of the animal she thinks you are referring to, have her stand up and say the animal's name and "It's my mother." Have that student remove her chair from the circle and sit in it while the game continues.

Post-reading Activity: Prior to this activity, moisten pairs of cotton balls with scents or extract, such as vanilla, lemon, vinegar, peppermint, or other scents you have available. Explain to students that most animals have a much better sense of smell than humans do. Many baby animals and mothers know each other by smell. Tell students that they will pretend to be baby animals looking for their mothers. The only catch is that they can only use their senses of smell, just like the animals, because they are going to be blindfolded! Put students in a circle. Give the scented cotton balls to the "mothers." Blindfold one student at a time and let her smell a scent that matches one of the scents held by the mothers. Tell each student that when it is her turn to be blindfolded, she must walk around the circle and sniff to find her "mother." Continue with this activity until each student has had a turn to act as the "mother" holding the cotton ball and also smell a scent and search for a "mother."

Name_____ Date _____

Color and cut out each animal below. Then, on another piece of paper, paste each mother animal next to her baby.

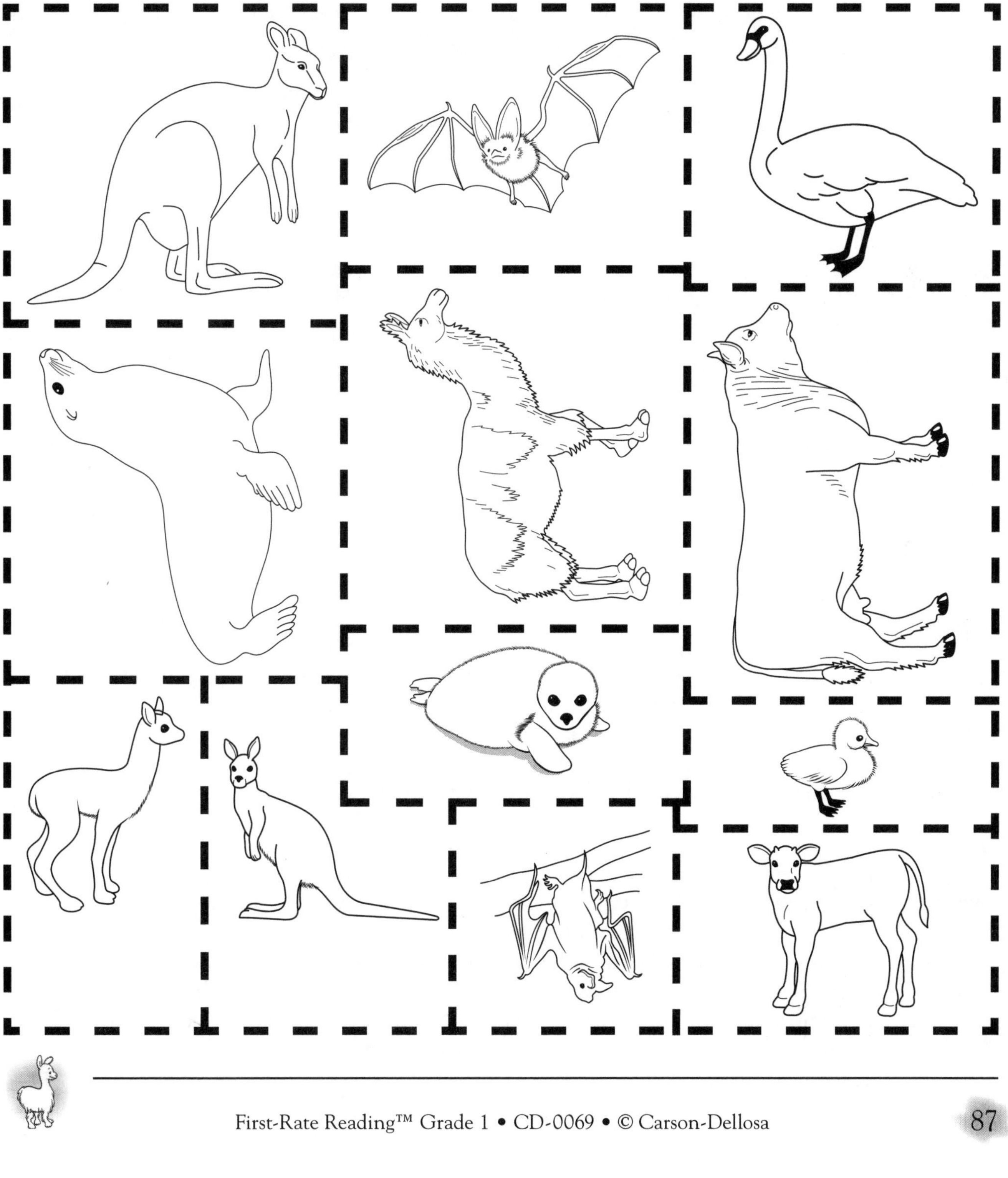

It Looked Like Spilt Milk

by Charles G. Shaw

(HarperCollins, 1947)

It Looked Like Spilt Milk peaks the reader's curiosity about what the shapes in the illustrations might be. In the end, the reader learns that all of the different forms on the pages are actually just clouds.

Related books: *The Cloud Book* by Tomie dePaola (Holiday House, 1985); *Little Cloud* by Eric Carle (Philomel, 1998)

Phonemic Awareness Activities
for *It Looked Like Spilt Milk*

Pre-reading Activity: Introduce the title *It Looked Like Spilt Milk*. Ask students to listen for the vowels as you say three of the words from the title: *it*, *spilt*, and *milk*. If they don't immediately hear the short /i/ sound, offer other words containing the short /i/ sound. (Note that the i's in *spilt* and *milk* are l-controlled and make a slightly different sound.) Then, say the word *like*. Ask students what vowel they hear in *like*. Remind students that the letter i has two sounds: short and long. Have students practice saying each sound. Play a substitution game with students. Ask them to listen as you say words with the short /i/ sound. Each time you say a word, ask them to change the short /i/ sound to the long /i/ sound to make another word. Say, "Bit, hit, lit, mitt, sit, kit, fit, knit." Students should respond, "Bite, height, light, might, sight, kite, fight, night." Explain that by changing the sound of the vowel, students can change a word to another word with a different meaning.

During-reading Activity: As you read the story, point out that the words *looked* and *like* are on each page. Ask students to identify the initial sound in each of these words. Inform them that there are many other places where they will hear the /l/ sound at the beginnings, middles, or ends of story words. Ask students to listen for /l/ sounds in words as you read. Tell each student to put up his thumb and index finger in the shape of an uppercase L when he hears a word with the sound. When students recognize a word, stop and let them repeat the word and identify in which part of the word they hear the /l/ sound.

Post-reading Activity: Initiate a lesson on rhyming words. Show the tree shape card from the Cloud Shapes reproducible (page 89) and ask if anyone can think of another shape that could be used in the story whose name rhymes with *tree*. (An answer might be *bee*.) Show the rest of the cards in random order so that students can identify all of the different shapes and pictures. Give each student either a picture card or a shape card. Have students with the shape cards spread out. Ask each student with a picture card to search for a student with a shape whose name rhymes with the name of her picture. Once students have found matches, have each group call out the rhyming words.

First-Rate Reading™ Grade 1 • CD-0069 • © Carson-Dellosa

Name_____ Date _____

Use the shape and picture cards with the phonemic awareness post-reading activity to help students play a rhyming game.

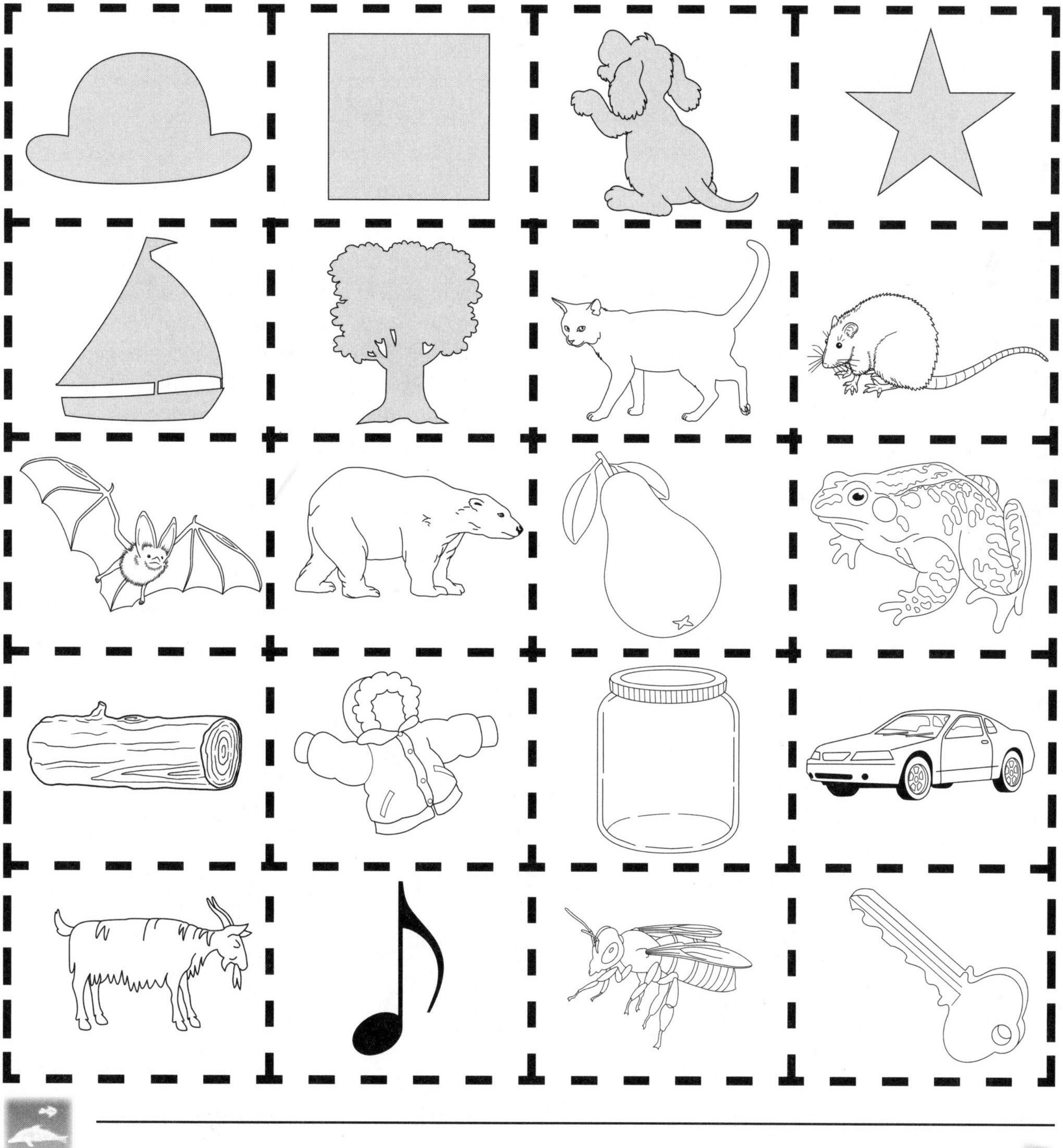

Phonics Activities
for *It Looked Like Spilt Milk*

Pre-reading Activity: The first word of the story title has two letters (*it*). Ask students if they can think of letters they can add to the letters it to make new words. Encourage students to think of blends and digraphs to add. Cut out a large cloud shape from white paper. As students offer suggestions, such as *hit*, *fit*, and *bit*, write the words on the cloud. Explain to students that what they did was create a word family. Tell students that in the story, there is a word that ends with ig. Make a new word family on another cloud shape for words ending in ig. Remind students that as they read the story with you, they should look to see if they wrote the ig word from the story (*pig*) on their cloud.

During-reading Activity: As you read the story, point out that the different shapes have names that begin with different initial letters. Ask students to say the sound at the beginning of each word. Give each student a piece of dark blue or black construction paper. Have her fold the paper in half as shown in step one of the Flap Book reproducible (page 91). Help each student draw three vertical lines on the top half of the paper to divide it into four sections. (See step two.) Ask each student to cut on the lines you have made from the edge of the paper to the middle (see step three). When she holds the paper with the fold at the top, she will now have four flip-up panels. Ask each student to select a name of a shape from the story and write the first letter of its name on the top of one panel. Repeat with the other three panels. Under each panel have her use a white or light yellow crayon to draw a shape whose name begins with the letter on the top panel, but is different from the shape in the book. Encourage students to use simple shapes. Have students share their flap books with other students in the class by saying the initial sounds they chose, then opening the flaps and saying the name of the shapes or pictures they drew. Allow classmates to guess what each student drew by calling out names of things that begin with the letter the student says before she shows and names her picture. This will give students another chance to practice recognizing letters and their sounds.

Post-reading Activity: Before beginning the activity, label seven open milk cartons or plastic cups with the consonant blends *sp, tr, cr, fl, gr, cl,* and *sk*. Then, cover a bulletin board with white batting and attach the cartons to the board with thumbtacks. Title the bulletin board "Cloud Clusters." Point out to students that there are many words in this story that begin with blends or consonant clusters. Remind students that a consonant cluster, or blend, is made of two consonants that keep their own sounds but blend together. Ask pairs to find these words in the story: *spilt, tree, cream, flower, great, cloud,* and *sky*. Help students find them, if necessary. On craft sticks, write all of the words students find. Have students sort the sticks by looking at the blends, saying the words, and dropping the sticks into the correct containers. Let students add to the game by creating additional blend containers and adding new words.

Name_____ Date _____

Use the directions below to create a flap book. Fold and cut a piece of construction paper as shown below.

1. Fold a piece of construction paper in half.

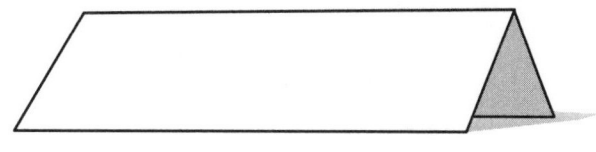

2. Draw three lines on the front flap to divide it into four panels.

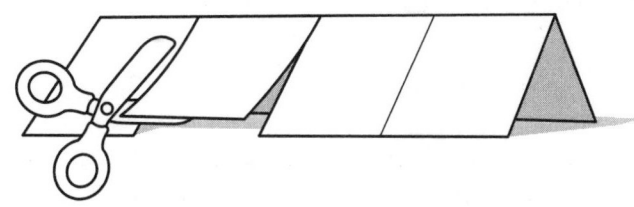

3. Cut along the lines you just drew. Stop cutting at the fold line.

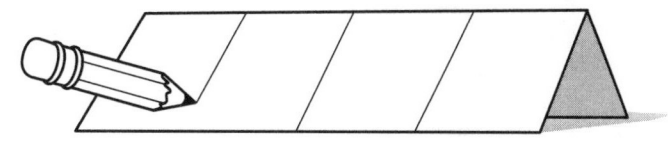

4. Write the first letter of a shape name from *It Looked Like Spilt Milk* on top of each panel. Underneath each panel, draw a picture of a shape that starts with that letter.

Vocabulary Activities
for *It Looked Like Spilt Milk*

Pre-reading Activity: Cut heavy paper into shapes similar to those in *It Looked Like Spilt Milk*. Have students look at the illustrations without reading the text. Ask them to try to identify each shape. Then, write the names of the shapes on the corresponding cutouts. This will give students visual clues to use to identify vocabulary words. As students review the vocabulary words, refer to the words on the shape cards and place them in a pocket chart or tape them to the board. Next, look through the book again and ask students if they recognize a word that may go with each picture in the book. If students don't recognize the words, ask them to sound out the words by looking first at the initial and final letters, and then any vowels in the words. Have them continue until they have matched each word to a picture. Finally, read the text to check their work.

During-reading Activity: As you read the story, talk about the different shapes in the illustrations and how the outlines of the shapes are not smooth. They look torn and have rough edges. To practice writing vocabulary words, ask each student to tear a piece of white paper so that it resembles a shape in the book. Have him glue the torn shape on blue paper and use a white crayon to copy the sentences from the page with the matching shape. Have each student use a fluorescent or light yellow crayon to underline any vocabulary words he finds especially difficult.

Post-reading Activity: A good way to practice vocabulary words is to give students a reason to memorize them by sight. Create a game from the Walk on Cloud Nine reproducible (page 93). Make at least 30 enlarged copies of the clouds. Write each of the following words and phrases on 16 clouds: *spilt, milk, bird, tree, ice cream, cone, flower, pig, birthday, cake, sheep, great horned owl, mitten, squirrel, angel, cloud*. Create several directional clouds such as *go back three spaces, miss a turn, move ahead one space,* etc., and several with the number nine. Laminate all clouds plus several blank clouds. Tape the clouds in a path around the classroom to create a game board. Have students use a spinner or roll a die to determine how many spaces to move. When a student lands on a cloud with a vocabulary word, have him say the word and define it. (Advanced students can also spell the words.) If a student incorrectly pronounces, defines, or spells a word, have him go back to the beginning cloud. If a student lands on a "cloud nine," give him a second turn. If he lands on a blank cloud, have him stay there until his next turn. Continue until someone reaches the end of the path. Reward students with milk and cookies or cotton candy—a cloud-like treat!

Name_____ Date _____

Make multiple, enlarged copies of the clouds, cut them out, and write vocabulary words and other directions on them to play the Walk on Cloud Nine game as described in the vocabulary post-reading activity.

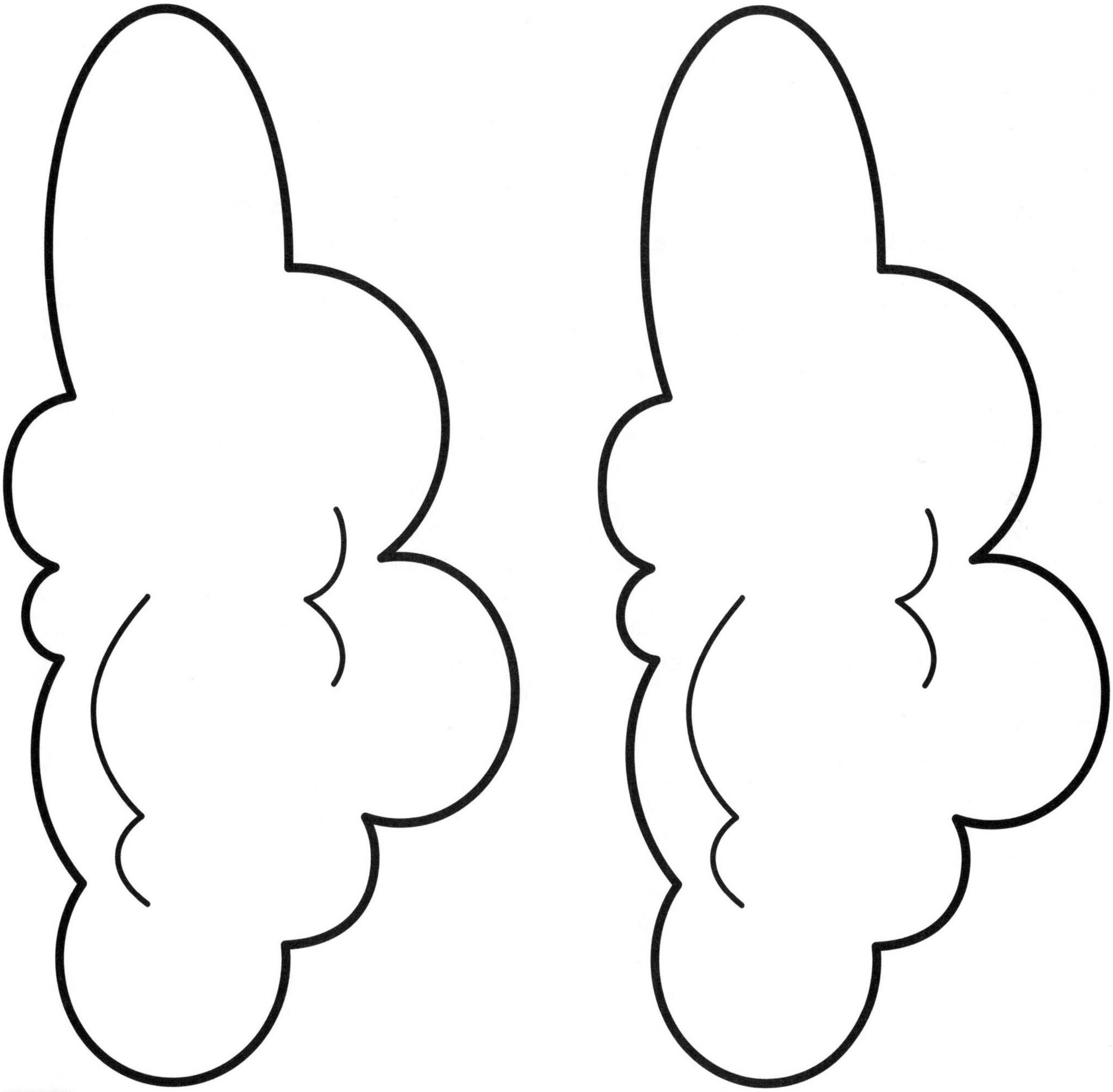

Fluency Activities

for *It Looked Like Spilt Milk*

Pre-reading Activity: Explain that some clouds, especially the big, fluffy kind, bring rain and sometimes thunderstorms. Provide students with the Boom, Bang! reproducible (page 95) so that they can practice *onomatopoeia*. Model how the poem should be read and have students recite it with you two more times. As they recite it, remind them that the sounds they make and the tones of their voices should reflect how it sounds and feels to be in a thunderstorm. Then, have students put motions to the lines to help them remember the words so that they can concentrate on fluency as they read the poem again. Have some students beat drums for the first two lines, then have others clap for the fourth line. Let students wave their hands back and forth for the fifth line and run in place for lines seven and eight.

During-reading Activity: Model how to read the simple story *It Looked Like Spilt Milk* by stressing some words in the sentences. In the first sentence on each page, stress the first word and the name of the shape. In each second sentence, stress the contraction and the name of the shape. On the last page, stress the middle word of the last sentence. As you read, point out to students what you are doing. Also, comment on how you stop between the sentences because of the periods. Ask students to read each page with you to learn how to read the story smoothly. Pair students to read together. You may want to pair accomplished readers with students who are having difficulty. Have them read different pages to each other as you visit each pair to monitor their progress. Make comments and corrections as you monitor. Have different pairs take turns reading the text to the class or to another class for added practice.

Post-reading Activity: Discuss with students how it is a little difficult to say *spilt milk* because the sounds are so similar. Help them create sentences with words that have similar sounds and write them on a piece of chart paper. Explain that most of the words in each sentence must contain similar sounds. Give them the examples, "Have no guilt over spilt milk," or "Mash and bash the trash for cash." Help students create more sentences like these using sounds from the story. Let them work in pairs to practice reading the sentences, then present them to the class, saying them five times fast.

Name_____ Date _____

Practice reading this poem aloud. Your teacher will tell you how to add motions to go with the words.

Loud Clouds

Crash, bang, sizzle, wham,
Grumble, bumble, grump!
Sing, zing, crack, bam,
Clattery, shattery, clump!
Wind sighs. Lightning sings!
Raindrops fall in a crowd.
Jump, run, storms are fun,
Take shelter from loud clouds!

Comprehension Activities
for *It Looked Like Spilt Milk*

Pre-reading Activity: Introduce the book by reading the title and looking at the shape on the cover. Ask students what the shape looks like to them. Most will recognize that the shape looks like a bird. Think aloud and say, "I wonder why the title of this book is *It Looked Like Spilt Milk?* Could the shape be milk that has spilled on a table?" Give students black or blue paper plates, tablespoons of whipped cream, and spoons or straws. Let students try to make shapes with their whipped cream. Then, give students a chance to respond with their ideas. Show students the illustrations in the book, but don't refer to the text. Ask what they see. They may respond that they see white shapes that look like animals and other things. Some of the shapes will be difficult for them to determine, but ask them to guess. Ask them where else they might see the shapes of objects but not really see the objects. Give them hints that they may see shapes outside. Place their predictions about the story on a piece of chart paper that has been cut to resemble the bird on the cover.

During-reading Activity: You'll need a sunny day with fluffy clouds for this activity. Read the text to students and refer back to the chart from the pre-reading activity (above). Ask students if their predictions about the story and the shapes were correct. Why or why not? Was the title useful in determining the content of the story? What were all of the shapes? Talk about clouds and how they can be different shapes, then demonstrate by walking outside and observing clouds. Have students draw pictures of the sky with clouds in the shapes they observe. Return to the classroom and give students time to color their pictures and glue cotton balls to the clouds. Have each student write a sentence about her cloud picture at the bottom of the page.

Post-reading Activity: After reading about clouds, provide small groups of students with easy, factual books about clouds and have them gather more information about the most common cloud forms: cirrus, cumulus, and stratus. Distribute the Cloud Types reproducible (page 97) for students to record their information. Allow students to illustrate the three types of clouds on the poster board and cut out the clouds. Encourage students to watch the sky for a few days to see if they can identify the different types of clouds. Ask students which type of cloud they think was pictured in *It Looked Like Spilt Milk*. (A cumulus cloud was shown, because cirrus and stratus are flatter clouds and don't make shapes like cumulus clouds do.)

Cloud Types
comprehension reproducible for
It Looked Like Spilt Milk

Name _____ Date _____

Look up cirrus, cumulus, and stratus clouds. Write the facts you find out on the clouds below. Cut out the clouds. Your teacher will tell you what to do next.

stratus clouds

cumulus clouds

cirrus clouds

The Itsy Bitsy Spider

by Iza Trapani

(Gareth Stevens Publishing, 1993)

Follow the spider through a favorite nursery rhyme as it climbs up a waterspout, and then finds other adventures and meets different characters. This story lends itself to teaching rhyme, action verbs, picture reading, and story innovation. Spiders' and other animals' characteristics and behaviors can also be taught.

Related books: *Creepy Crawlies A to Z* by Louisa Ainsworth (Scholastic Professional Books, 2000); *Rain* by Robert Kalan (HarperTrophy, 1991); *The Very Busy Spider* by Eric Carle (Philomel Books, 1995)

Phonemic Awareness Activities
for *The Itsy Bitsy Spider*

Pre-reading Activity: If students know the song, sing the *Itsy Bitsy Spider* with them. Ask them to listen as you say *itsy* slowly. Ask them to listen for the first vowel sound. Give examples of other short /i/ words. Say the word *spider* slowly. Ask them to identify the first vowel sound. Say other words with the long /i/ sound. Read the poem from the Spin Spider Spin reproducible (page 99) to students. Ask what vowel sounds they hear in the words *spin*, *time*, *sit*, and *right*. Then have students say the poem with you. Ask them to listen as you repeat the poem again, but this time ask them to make a flicking motion with their fingers when they hear a word with a short /i/ sound and wiggle hands like a spider when they hear a word with a long /i/ sound.

During-reading Activity: Give each student a rubber spider and a piece of string. Let students tie their strings around the spiders. (Students can also make spiders from wiggly eyes, string, and pom-poms or paper.) Explain to students that they should dangle the spiders when they hear a word in the story with a long /i/ sound like in the word *spider*. Read the story to students and see how many words they hear that contain the long /i/ sound.

Post-reading Activity: Play a spider game similar to "Duck, Duck, Goose." Have students sit in a circle. Select a student to be the spider. Have the spider walk around the outside of the circle and tap each student on the shoulder while repeating the words *itsy, bitsy*. At some point, the student should tap someone and say *spider*. The tapped student must run around the circle and try to get back to his seat before getting tagged by the "spider." If tagged, the student must answer whether a story word you call out has a long or short /i/ sound. If he answers incorrectly, have him go to the center of the circle until the game is finished. If not tagged, have the student sit in the same seat and have the "spider" answer. If the "spider" answers incorrectly, have her go to the center of the circle, and make the student who ran around the circle the new "spider." Continue until everyone has had a chance to answer.

Name_____ Date _____

Read the poem to students. Ask them to make a flicking motion when they hear a word with a short /i/ sound and wiggle their hands like spiders when they hear a word with a long /i/ sound.

Spin, spin, spin, spider,
Spin, spin, spin.
Spin, spin, spin, spider,
Spin, spin, spin.
In and out,
Up and down,
Around and about.

Weave, weave, weave, spider,
Weave, weave, weave.
Weave, weave, weave, spider,
Weave, weave, weave.
In and out,
Up and down,
Around and about.

Rest, rest, rest, spider,
Rest, rest, rest.
Rest, rest, rest, spider,
Rest, rest, rest.
Take time out,
Sit right down,
Around and about.

Phonics Activities
for *The Itsy Bitsy Spider*

re-reading Activity: Explain to students that in *The Itsy, Bitsy Spider*, there are many words that begin with consonant blends (clusters). Remind students that the two letters in a blend retain their own sounds when blended. Write the following story words on index cards and show each one to students: *climbed, swoosh, plopped, slipped, spin, flicked, stop, creep, dry, blow,* and *try.* Ask students to say the blend at the beginning of each word and use their decoding skills to sound out the rest of the word. After reviewing each word, divide each card by cutting a jagged, curved, or diagonal line between the blend and the rest of the word. Scramble the cut cards and ask students to take turns putting the cards together again to find the words.

uring-reading Activity: Prior to this activity, print lowercase a's, e's, i's, o's, and u's on a set of wooden clothespins. (Make about five clothespins for each vowel.) As you read the first few pages of the story, ask students what they notice about the words that end the sentences. Lead them to the conclusion that the story is told in verse and that certain words rhyme. Ask students to name and point to the words in the story that rhyme. Have multiple copies of the book available. Pair students, and give each pair a set of clothespins and a copy of the Spider Rhymes reproducible (page 101). Have them cut out the spiders. Ask the pairs to read through the book to find the words on the spiders. Have each pair clip a clothespin to the spider to find the correct vowel. (Since there is only one of each vowel, they should be able to eliminate incorrect words by using the book for reference.) Have students color the spiders. Create a bulletin board with five webs made of string, and attach the spiders according to the vowels in the words on them. For example, put all of the short /a/ spiders on one web, all of the short /e/ spiders on another web, etc. Save the bulletin board and the clothespins for the post-reading activity.

ost-reading Activity: Inform students that in the text of *The Itsy Bitsy Spider*, there are many words that contain short vowels. Say words with short vowel sounds. Ask students to repeat the words and then the sounds. On index cards, write words from the story that have short vowel sounds such as *and, ran, cat, back, rested, went, when, then, fell, kitchen, with, in, flicked, itsy, bitsy, did, it, silky, plopped, on, top, spun, jumped, washed, sun, fan, his, knocked, slipped, stop,* and *up.* Leave the spaces for the short vowels blank. Show the cards to students and explain that a vowel is missing in each word. Ask students to think of what the words might be and clip the vowel clothespins in the spaces where the vowels should be to spell the words correctly. Then, create an interactive bulletin board game with the cards and clothespins. Leave the short vowel spiders on the web from the during-reading activity. Place all of the cards in an envelope attached to the board. Have students practice making words by attaching the cards to the web with the clothespins.

Name _____ Date _____

Cut out the spiders. Each spider has a rhyming story word with a missing vowel. Find each word in the book, then use a clothespin to attach the correct vowel. When you are finished, take off each clothespin and write the correct vowel on the line. Color the spiders.

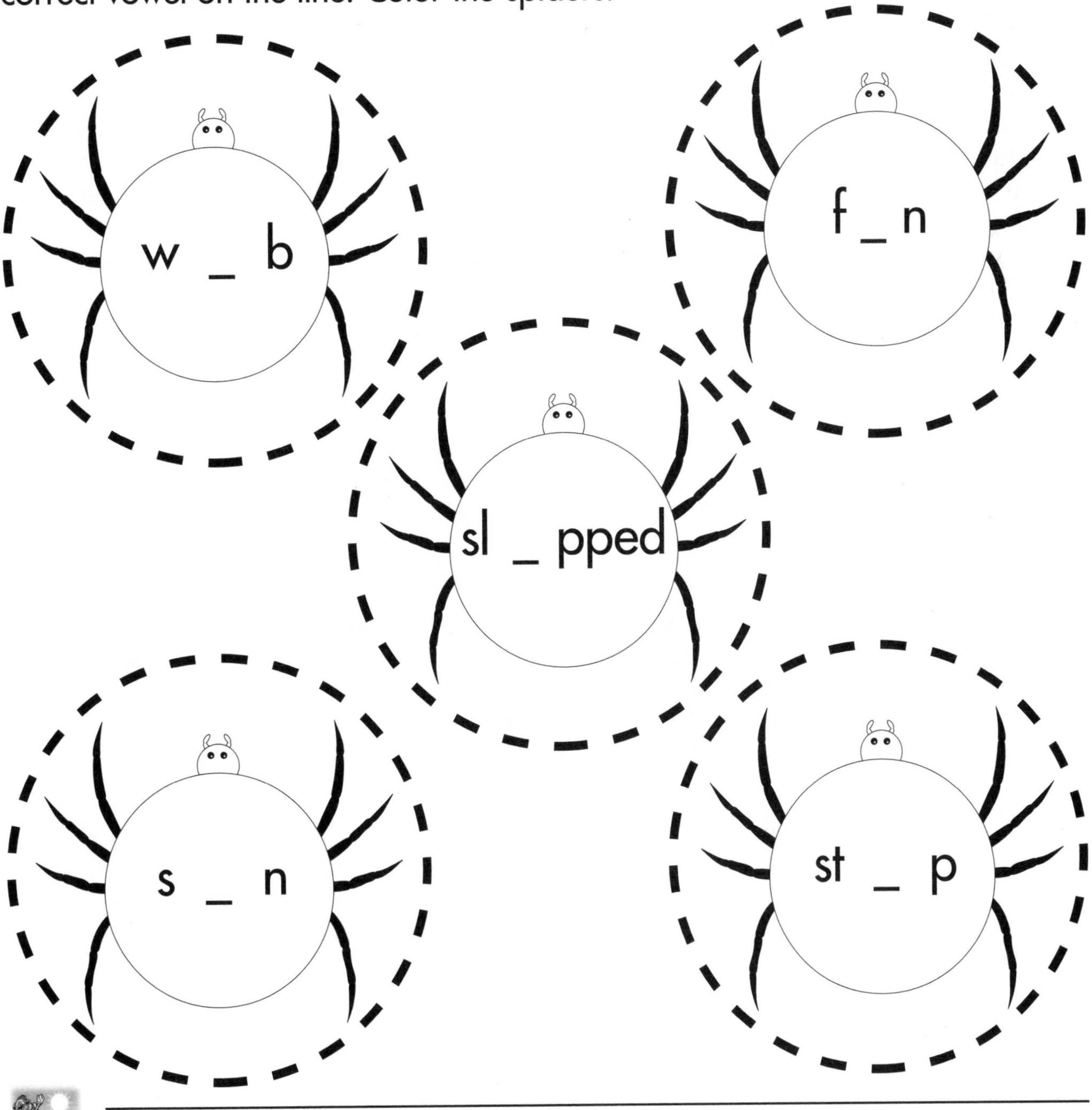

w _ b

f _ n

sl _ pped

s _ n

st _ p

Vocabulary Activities
for *The Itsy Bitsy Spider*

re-reading Activity: Explain that there are many action verbs in this story. Some of these words have the suffix ed added to them. Show students the following words: *climbed, washed, flicked, knocked, plopped, slipped,* and *rested.* Have them find the base word in each word. Explain that in the words *plopped* and *slipped,* besides removing the ed, the second p must also be removed to leave only the base word. Ask a volunteer to explain what each word means by acting it out. Ask students to add other endings to the words. They will discover that an s, es, or ing can be added to each word to change the time of the action. Introduce two other words from the story: *creep* and *swoosh.* Demonstrate that ing and s or es can be added to these words as well. Also, explain that when adding endings to some words, the final consonant in the base word must be doubled. Have students play a game of Tic-Tac-Toe to practice recognizing the words. Provide pairs of students with copies of the Tic-Tac-Toe reproducible (page 103), and sets of index cards with action words written on each card. Instruct each player to select an index card, then place a marker on the same word on the reproducible. When a student has covered three words in a row, he must then use each word in a sentence and also demonstrate the action of each word to prove that he knows the meanings of the words. Let students play with different classmates until students understand all of the words.

uring-reading Activity: As you read the story aloud, have students find the action words to discover to whom or what the action belonged. Ask, "Who climbed? Who was washed out? Who flicked? What knocked the spider? Who plopped? Who slipped? Who rested? Who crept and spun?" Let students sing the song and act out the actions as they sing. Observe students carefully as they act to make sure they know what the words mean.

ost-reading Activity: Ask each student to select an action word from the story and draw a picture of the word. Have students label the drawings and write sentences containing the action verbs. Write verbs on the index cards, then post the pictures on a bulletin board under the appropriate cards. Add the action words to a classroom word wall for future reference.

Tic-Tac-Toe
vocabulary reproducible for
The Itsy Bitsy Spider

Name _____   Date _____

Use a set of word cards with these words written on them. Play with a partner. Take turns choosing word cards. Put a game piece on each word you turn over. If you get three in a row, use each word in a sentence and demonstrate the action to win the game.

climbed	washed	flicked
rested	plopped	knocked
crept	slipped	swooshed

Fluency Activities
for *The Itsy Bitsy Spider*

Pre-reading Activity: Ask students to sing the song "The Itsy Bitsy Spider." Most students will recognize this familiar tune, but refer to the last page of the book if they are unfamiliar with it. Add hand motions for each verse. Perform the song for a class of younger students, and allow your class to teach them the song and hand motions. Post an enlarged copy of the last page to help students remember the long verses.

During-reading Activity: Unlike the original song, in this version, the spider continues to climb up other things. The spider climbs up five different things in the story, and unfortunately, she needs to climb up everything twice. Divide students into five groups and have them read the different portions of the story that refer to the things the spider climbs. Remind them to read the story as smoothly as they can. Provide multiple copies of the book and give students time to practice. Monitor the groups and offer suggestions for how to say the lines and pause at appropriate times. When students are ready, have each group read its portion of the story to the rest of the class. Then, have the entire class read the story chorally.

Post-reading Activity: Continue teaching fluency with a kinesthetic twist. Have students read the Adventures in Motion reproducible (page 105) and underline all of the action words in the story. Remind students that they will not become fluent readers if they read word by word, so ask them to make up motions as a class to perform along with the poem. Explain that the motions will help them remember what words come next and will contribute to the fluent reading of the story. Next to the lines of the poem, have students draw or make notes for each motion. Slowly go over the motions of the story as you read the words, letting the class follow along. Repeat the story several times, reading and moving a little faster each time. Speed up the poem and motions until they are hard to understand. Ask students if a listener would understand the poem at this pace. Then, read the poem and perform the motions as a class, slowing down the words and movements so that they are at a comfortable pace.

Name _____   Date _____

Practice the following poem and put motions to the poem to help you remember it.

Run through the desert,
Swim in the sea!
Around and about,
Around and about.

Slide down a mountain,
Climb up a tree!
Around and about,
Around and about,

Over and under,
And in and out.
Around and about,
Around and about!

Comprehension Activities
for *The Itsy Bitsy Spider*

Pre-reading Activity: Students who are familiar with *The Itsy Bitsy Spider* will be delighted when you inform them that there is more to the story. Show them the book and review the title and cover illustration. Explain that the name on the cover is the person who is retelling the story. *The Itsy Bitsy Spider*, like many other rhymes, is so old that the real author's name is unknown. Since you cannot share much information about where the story originated, ask students to tell you what they know about spiders such as what they look like, how many legs they have, whether they lay eggs, kinds of food they eat, where they are found, and of course, information about the webs they spin. As students describe spiders, write their comments on a piece of chart paper. Title it *Spider Specifics*. Inform students that they will be reading a story about *The Itsy Bitsy Spider*. In the story, besides climbing up the waterspout, the spider visits four new places. Ask them to guess where the four new places might be, then verify where the spider goes during the story.

During-reading Activity: Open the book so that students can see the front and back covers, and ask them to look carefully at how the cat is peering at the spider with one eye. Ask them what the cat might be thinking as it watches the spider spin its web. There are many other characters in the story that interact with the spider, although most of them are never mentioned in the text. As you read the story aloud, point out the other creatures such as the butterfly, turtle, salamander, frogs, mouse, bird, bee, cat (when it is jumping), chipmunk, rabbit, etc. Discuss whether the animals are looking at the spider and what they might be thinking. Some animals seem interested, while others don't notice the spider. Assign each student an animal, and have her write or dictate a few sentences about what her animal is thinking in the story.

Post-reading Activity: Explain to students that just as Iza Trapani added to the story, they can add more verses, too. Explain that the act of adding to a story is called *innovation*. The story ends with the itsy bitsy spider taking a rest in her web. Ask students to think about what the spider might do after her nap. Refer to the *Spider Specifics* chart from the pre-reading activity above, then have students determine how they want to continue the story. Have each student write her rhyme on the body of the spider on the More Spider Adventures reproducible (page 107), cut out the spider, and then glue it to a paper plate. Attach a string to the top and bottom of each spider plate. String students' plates together and hang them on a bulletin board or in a window.

Name_____ Date _____

Write a verse on the pattern about the next place the itsy bitsy spider goes. Cut out the pattern and glue it to a paper plate.

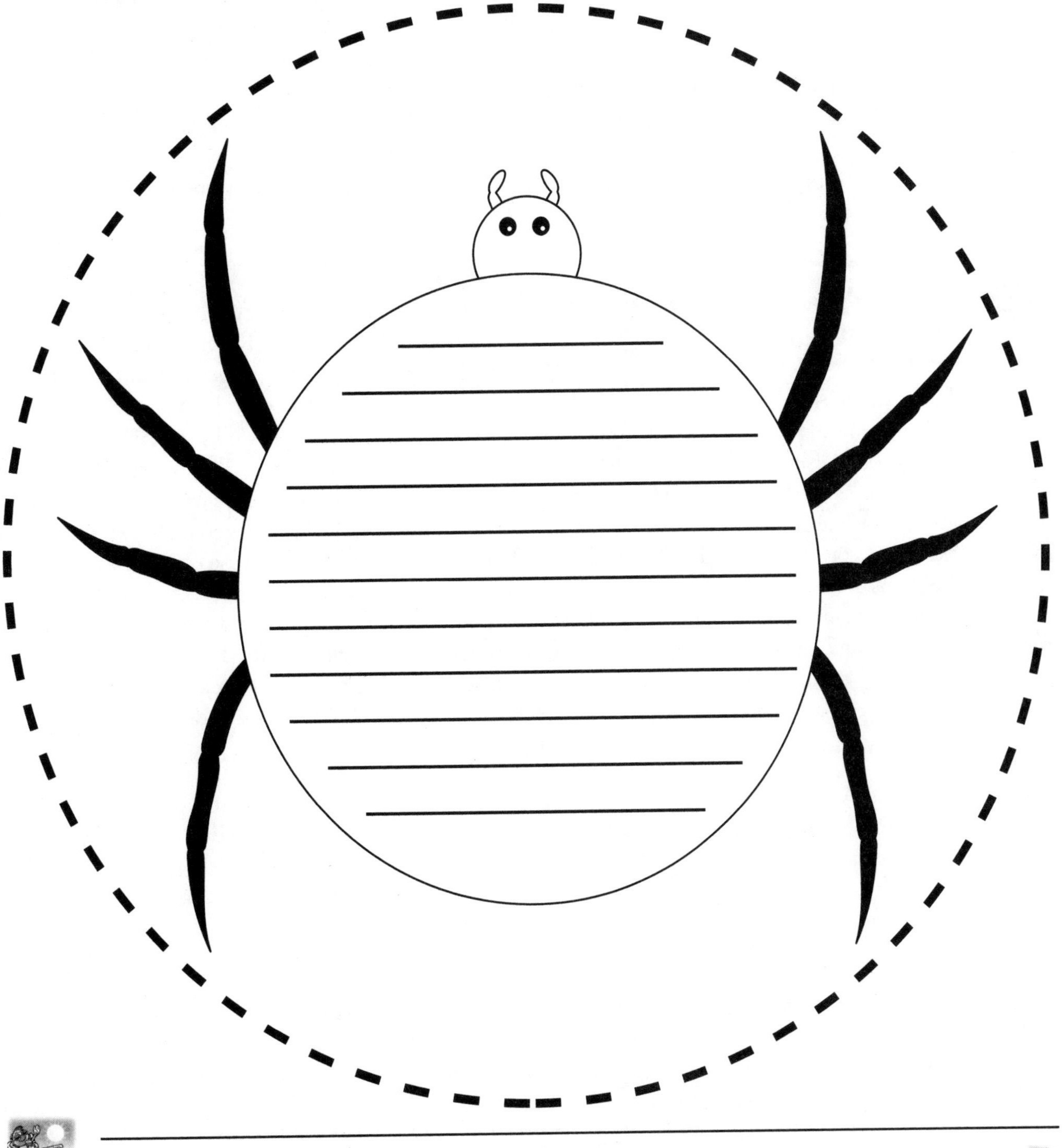

Jamaica's Find

by Juanita Havill
(Houghton Mifflin, 1986)

Jamaica finds a stuffed dog in a park and is torn between keeping it for herself and returning it to the park's Lost and Found. Children will empathize with Jamaica and her struggle to do the right thing. This book can be used to teach word endings, contractions, character analysis, and making choices.

Related books: *Lilly's Purple Plastic Purse* by Kevin Henkes (Greenwillow, 1996); *Tyrone the Double Dirty Rotten Cheater* by Hans Wilhelm (Scholastic, 1991)

Phonemic Awareness Activities
for *Jamaica's Find*

Pre-reading Activity: Have students make badges from the Ending Experts reproducible (page 109) to use for all three phonemic awareness activities. Tape them to students' shirts. Tell students that they are going to read a book about a little girl who finds things. Say the word *find*. Ask students what sound they hear at the end of *find* (/nd/). Ask what two letters make that sound. Repeat with the base word for *pumping*, which is *pump* (/mp/). Tell students that they are going to become "ending experts" by identifying which words have certain endings. Have students form a line. Explain that you are going to say a word to the first person in line and he should listen for the ending sound /nd/. If he hears that sound at the end of the word, he should say, "The end," and go to the end of the line. If he doesn't hear that sound at the end of the word, he should say, "It's not over," and wait for another word. Use these words to play the game: *mind, hand, mad, pound, find, ground, fad, blind, found, brown, pond, hound, hour, count, sand, vent, around, wait, want, behind, red, blond,* and *round*. Play the game again, this time telling students to listen for the /mp/ sound at the ends of the words. Use the words *jump, gym, pump, limp, job, shrimp, clap, flap, scamp, damp, road, ramp, log, lump, map, cramp, cram, stamp, lap, lamp, tap, top, tramp, trap,* and *slump*.

During-reading Activity: Tape Ending Experts badges to students' shirts. Show students *Jamaica's Find* and read the title to them. Tell the "ending experts" to listen for /nt/ as in *front*, /ld/ as in *held*, /nd/ as in *find*, and /mp/ as in *jump*. Write the endings on the board. As you read the story aloud, they should say "The end" each time they hear one of these sounds at the end of a word. Students should say "The end" to the following words: *pump, front, round, behind, sand, found, held, around,* and *want*.

Post-reading Activity: Once again, tape Ending Experts badges to students' shirts. Tell students that they will be changing word endings. Review the ending sounds from the last two activities (/nt/, /mp/, /ld/, and /nd/). Have students change the words containing these endings by deleting specific letters. For example, ask students to say *went* without the /t/ and to say *find* without the /d/.

Name_____ Date_____

Color and cut out the badge below. Tape the badge to your shirt to become an expert at hearing word endings.

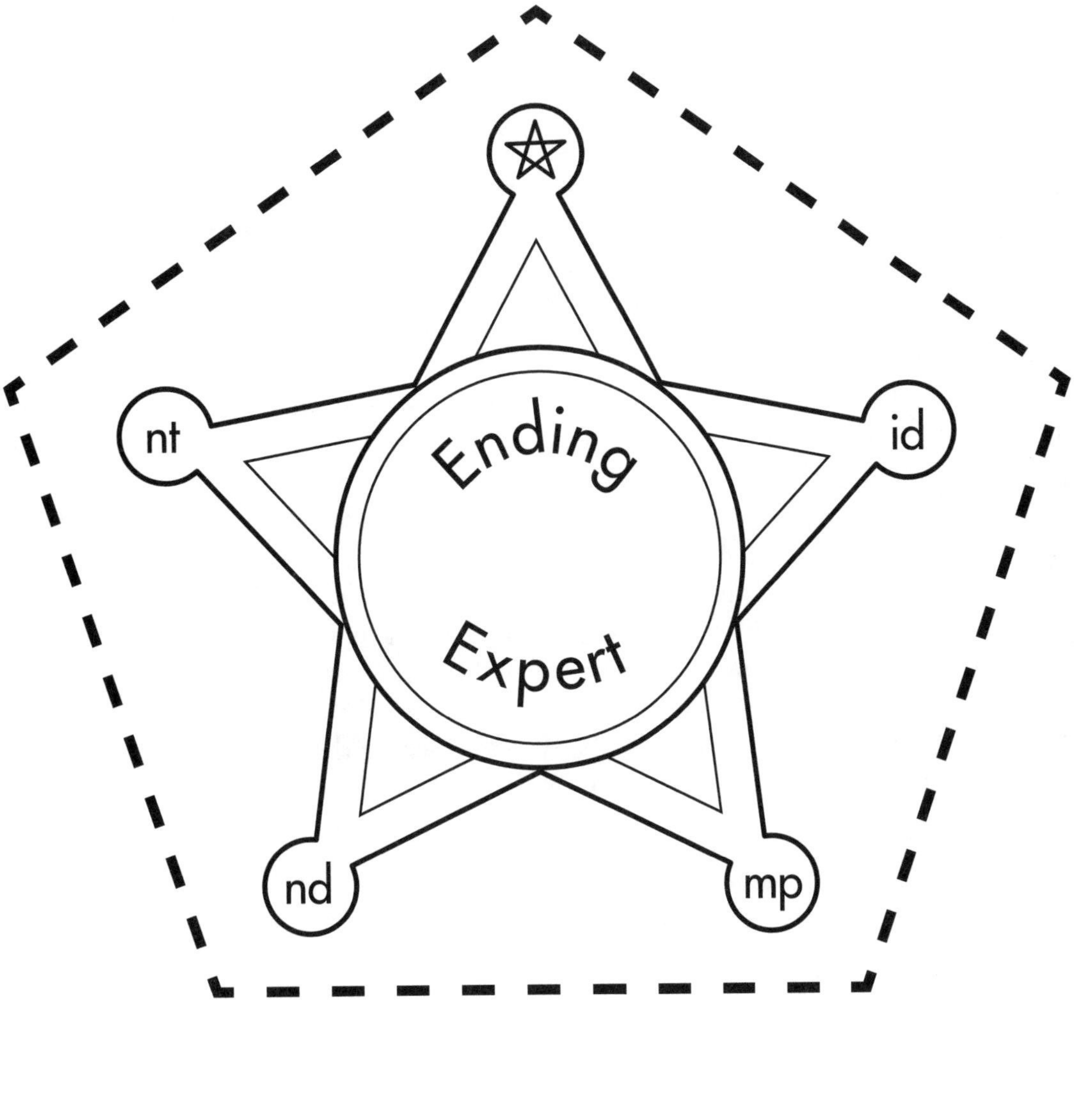

nt

id

Ending

Expert

nd

mp

Phonics Activities
for *Jamaica's Find*

Pre-reading Activity: Introduce the main character, Jamaica, to students by writing her name on the board. Ask students what sound the letter c makes in her name (/k/). Write the following story words on the board: *climbed, cuddly, bicycle, counter, clean, closely, called,* and *come*. Review the words aloud and have students read them to decide in which words the c makes the /k/ sound and in which it makes the /s/ sound. List each sound next to its word. Then, help students brainstorm more soft and hard c words.

During-reading Activity: Show students the book cover. Draw attention to the title and ask what vowels make a long /a/ sound in *Jamaica* (ai). Have students brainstorm other words that have the ai vowel team. Explain that in most cases, when certain vowels are together, the first one usually "says its name" and the second one is silent. Teach the mnemonic device, "When two vowels go walking, the first one does the talking." List other vowel combinations that do this such as ea as in *neat*, oa as in *boat*, and ue as in *blue*. (The u doesn't exactly "say its name," but it makes the /oo/ sound.) When you read the book *Jamaica's Find*, pause at the words *toes, either, chair, squeezed, feeling,* and *ears*. Ask students to name which vowel "walks" and which "talks" in each word. Also, explain exceptions like *round, head, house, young, doesn't, said*, etc.

Post-reading Activity: After the during-reading activity, when students have grasped the concept of vowel teams (the first vowel "saying its name" and the second vowel remaining silent), review exceptions to this rule again. Pair students and assign each pair a page or two of the book. Give each pair a copy of the Vowel Team Raindrops reproducible (page 111) and several index cards. Have students search their assigned pages for words with vowel teams. If they find a word containing a vowel team that follows the rule, have them write the word on a raindrop. (Remind them that *rain* is an example of the rule.) If students find a word containing a vowel team that is an exception, have them write it on an index card. Review the words that students find and make any corrections. Then, let them brainstorm their own vowel team words and write them either on index cards or raindrops. Have students lightly color their raindrops blue. Post the reproducibles on a bulletin board and create the border by attaching the index cards around the perimeter. Title the bulletin board "It's Raining Vowel Teams!"

Vowel Team Raindrops

phonics reproducible for
Jamaica's Find

Name_____ Date _____

In each raindrop, write a word that contains a vowel team. Make sure that the words you choose follow the rule, "When two vowels go walking, the first one does the talking." Cut out the raindrops.

Vocabulary Activities
for *Jamaica's Find*

Pre-reading Activity: Tell students that they are going to go on a vocabulary search. Their mission is to find words that end in ed or ing. Divide students into two groups. Assign a "writer" to each group. Have one group find ed words and the other group find ing words in the book. When students finish, bring them back together and create a list of the words they found. Discuss what type of words these are (verbs). Students should find the following words: *arrived, stuffed, returned, pushed, climbed, rolled, feeling, stopped, looked, stayed, plopped, smiled, squeezed, answered, called, tossed, pumping, hugging, shouting, bending, playing,* and *watching.* Keep this list on display for students to refer to when reading the story.

During-reading Activity: Review with students the vocabulary list from the pre-reading activity. Tell students to continue their vocabulary search as you read the book. Each time they hear a word that has an ed or an ing ending they should raise their hands and be prepared to act out the word. For example, if students hear the word *squeezed,* they should show what the word means by squeezing either themselves or something else. Read the story slowly to allow time for students to hear the words and then raise their hands. Continue in this manner until you have finished the story. Then, have each student choose two words from the pre-reading list and draw pictures of someone or something performing those actions. (Each student should draw one picture on each side of her page.) Ask students to write the words they are drawing in the lower corners of the papers. Have students stand at the front of the classroom and show their pictures. Have them select volunteers to guess the verbs.

Post-reading Activity: Pretend that Kristen, the owner of the stuffed dog, loses him again. The lost stuffed dog is going to have wild adventures and students are going to write the stories! Display the vocabulary list from the pre-reading activity. Hand out the Lost Dog Adventures reproducible (page 113). Tell students that they will fill in the blanks with the vocabulary words. Explain that there are no right or wrong answers as long as the stories makes sense. Have students share stories when they are finished. Point out the different places students used certain vocabulary words or determine which word was most popular for each blank. To make this activity easier, copy the story on a transparency and fill it in as a class by letting volunteers suggest appropriate vocabulary words from the list. Alternately, use the page as an "ad-libs" page. Ask students to state random words that end in ed or ing. Write in their answers and share the silly story that results.

Lost Dog Adventures
vocabulary reproducible for
Jamaica's Find

Name_____ Date _____

Use the vocabulary list below to help you complete this story. Write the words in the blanks.

stuffed	rolled	shouting	stopped	looked	watching
stayed	feeling	tossed	climbed	squeezed	dropped
looked	playing	squeezed	hugging	feeling	

The _____Dog

Kristin was so busy playing that she did not see that her stuffed

dog _____ down a hill. He was _____

to Kristin, but she didn't hear him. He _____

shouting and _____ at a big dog who was

_____ him. He _____ very still. The big

dog was _____ playful so he _____ the

stuffed dog high in the air. The big dog _____

to the top of the hill with the stuffed dog_____

between his teeth. He _____ him on the ground and

_____ around. Just then, Kristin saw her stuffed dog.

She stopped _____ and ran to him. She picked him up

and _____ him hard. She kept _____

him all the way home. The stuffed dog was very tired, but he was

_____ very loved.

The End

Fluency Activities
for *Jamaica's Find*

Pre-reading Activity: Tell students that reading with fluency takes knowledge and practice. Explain that most adults practice when they need to read in front of an audience. Often, people practice in front of friends or family in order to become familiar with the words. Make some tools to help students read more fluently. Show them a picture of a traffic light or draw one on the board. Ask students where they have seen that object before and if they can name what each color of light means. Talk about when a reader might need to go or speed up and when a reader might need to slow down or stop. Ask students which punctuation marks they could match to each traffic light color. Help students connect a red light to a period, question mark, or exclamation point; a yellow light to a comma; and a green light to an uppercase letter at the beginning of a sentence. (You may want to point out the difference between these and uppercase letters at the beginnings of proper nouns and periods used in abbreviations.) Hand out the Reading Lights reproducible (page 115). Have each student color the stop circle red, the pause circle yellow, and the go circle green. Let students cut out the circles and attach craft sticks to each to make handles. Tell students that instead of traffic lights, they have just made "reading lights." Like real traffic lights, these can be used to tell students to go, slow down, or stop. Use the reading lights in the during-reading activity.

During-reading Activity: Discuss how it feels to ride in a car. Talk about how most of the time a ride is very smooth. Talk about what happens when a car stops suddenly. Talk about how awful a car ride would be if the car started, stopped, started, stopped, started, and stopped. Explain to students that if they do not read fluently, they are just like that car! (You may want to demonstrate by having students walk in a line, and abruptly telling them to stop and go.) Read the story in a small group setting so that students can be close enough to actually see the punctuation and uppercase letters in the text. Have them hold up the reading lights as they see punctuation and uppercase letters while you read aloud. Read slowly to allow students time to raise their lights at appropriate places.

Post-reading Activity: Have students read to partners for this activity. Assign pages in the text for students to read orally. Assign struggling readers pages with little text. Ask one student in each pair to hold up the correct colors of reading lights while the other student reads the page. Then, have them switch jobs and read again. Give students ample time to practice reading their pages before reading in front of the class. Students will be forced to pay attention to punctuation marks in order to give their partners time to raise the appropriate lights.

First-Rate Reading™ Grade 1 • CD-0069 • © Carson-Dellosa

Reading Lights
fluency reproducible for
Jamaica's Find

Name _____ Date _____

Color the circle with ending punctuation red. Color the circle with the comma yellow. Color the circle with the words Uppercase Letter green. Cut out the circles and tape craft sticks to them to make handles. Instead of traffic lights, you have just created "reading lights." Hold them up to show punctuation as you read.

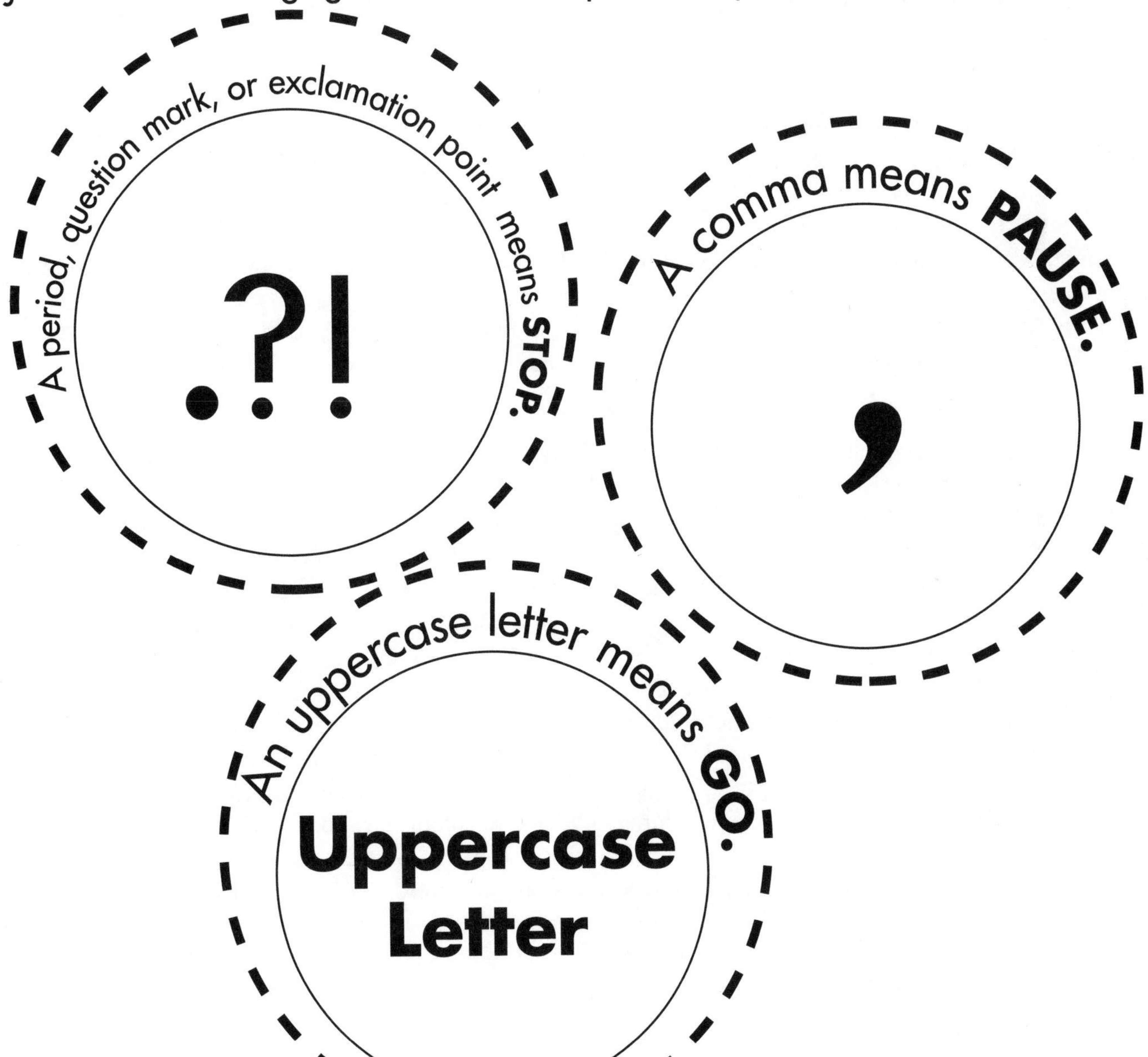

A period, question mark, or exclamation point means **STOP.**

. ? !

A comma means **PAUSE.**

,

An uppercase letter means **GO.**

Uppercase Letter

Comprehension Activities

for *Jamaica's Find*

Pre-reading Activity: Show students the book cover and read the title aloud. Tell students that Jamaica finds three things in this story. Ask students to predict what Jamaica finds. Write their answers on a piece of chart paper. Ask students to predict from the picture what Jamaica is like and to give you reasons for their predictions. Write their answers on the chart. Explain to students that sometimes people have choices to make and that in this story Jamaica has a choice to make. Ask students to predict what kind of choice Jamaica might have to make and to give reasons why. Again, add their predictions to the chart. Refer to this chart after you have read the story to students.

During-reading Activity: Explain that Jamaica, the little girl in the story, has many different feelings as the story unfolds. Tell students to listen closely to the story to decide how Jamaica feels at the beginning, in the middle, and at the end of the story. Read the story to students. Refer back to the predictions students made in the pre-reading activity. Discuss whether their predictions were accurate. Why or why not? What was the third thing Jamaica found? (Possible answers could be a friend, happiness, or a good feeling.) Hand out the Jamaica's Finds reproducible (page 117). Depending on students' levels, either have them complete this activity individually, in pairs, or in groups. Ask students how they think Jamaica felt in the beginning, middle, and end of the story.

Post-reading Activity: Explain that Jamaica had a decision to make in this story. Lead a discussion about the decision. Discuss how Jamaica really liked the dog she found, but when she heard her mother say that the dog probably belonged to a little girl just like Jamaica, she was no longer happy. Ask students, "Why? What was the decision Jamaica had to make? What did she decide? Was it the right decision? What would you have decided to do?" Tell students that they are going to practice making choices. Divide students into groups. Assign a scenario to each group. Have each student take a part and role-play the scene for the class. Conduct a class discussion about the decision made after each group performs. Use the following scenarios: (1) Jimmy doesn't know an answer on a test, but he can see his friend's paper. What does Jimmy do? (2) Lucy forgot her homework for the third day in a row. Her teacher might call her mom or dad, and she wouldn't be allowed to watch TV for a week. She asks her friend, Joey, if she can copy his homework. What does Joey do? (3) Micaela doesn't like the school lunches, which she buys every day. She never eats more than one bite. Her lunch aide says he might have to call her mom, but Micaela begs him not to because she knows how busy her mom is with her job. She doesn't have time to make lunch in the morning. The lunch aide tells Micaela that she has two days to do something about this problem. What does Micaela do? (4) Brianna really wants to play with Harry and Susan at recess every day, but when she tries to play with them, they tell her that she has to give them money. Even though Brianna has change from her lunch money, she doesn't know if she should give it to them. What does Brianna do?

Jamaica's Finds
comprehension reproducible for
Jamaica's Find

Name_____ Date _____

Finish the three sentence starters to tell what happened in the beginning, middle, and end of the story *Jamaica's Find*.

BEGINNING

In the first part of the story, Jamaica was

_____ because

_____ .

MIDDLE

In the middle of the story, Jamaica was

_____ because

_____ .

END

At the end of the story, Jamaica was

_____ because

_____ .

Livingstone Mouse

by Pamela Duncan Edwards

(HarperCollins, 1996)

Young Livingstone Mouse realizes that finding a new home is hard, but his determination to succeed leads to a happy ending. The beautiful illustrations show the world from a different perspective. Use this book to teach syllabication, verbs, suffixes, and sequence.

Related books: *The Mouse and the Motorcycle* by Beverly Cleary (HarperTrophy, 1990); *Mouse Mess* by Linnea Asplind Riley (Scholastic, 1997)

Phonemic Awareness Activities
for *Livingstone Mouse*

Pre-reading Activity: Tell students that some of the words in Livingstone Mouse are "eee-noooor-mous." Ask students to put the syllables together into a word. Divide the class into two groups. Read large story words slowly. Have students blend the syllables to guess the following words: *Livingstone, investigating, announced, murmured, somersaults, complaining, cockroaches, argumentative, majestically, fantastic, peculiar, entrance, screeched, scurried, shuddering, everywhere, moonlight,* and *glistening.* Alternate teams and exaggerate each syllable and sound. Review vowel and consonant sounds students should already know. The students on the team with the most correct guesses are the "enormous word champions!"

During-reading Activity: Remind students that words are made of syllables. Have students raise their hands as they hear words from the pre-reading activity. Stop reading and have a student say the word syllable by syllable. If no one raises his hand for a word, skip over it and continue to read. After reading, challenge students to recall some of the larger words and say them syllable by syllable. Have the class count syllables to determine which words had the most syllables (*investigation, argumentative,* and *majestically*). Ask if students know other enormous words. As they respond, have the class count syllables. Can they think of words with more than five syllables?

Post-reading Activity: Draw a large stop sign on the board. Underline the letters st in the word *stop*. Have students read the word. Ask what sound the underlined letters make. Explain that the letters st are a blend. A consonant blend has two consonants that stand side by side in a word, but each consonant make its own sound. Give a craft stick and a copy of the Stop for Blends reproducible (page 119) on card stock to each student. Have each student color and cut out her stop sign, then tape a craft stick to the bottom for a handle. Explain that this book has many words with the st consonant blend. Each time they hear the /st/ sound, they should hold up their stop signs. When they hold up their signs, ask a volunteer to name the word and tell whether the st is in the beginning, middle, or end of the word. Save the stop signs for the phonics post-reading activity.

Name _____ Date _____

Color and cut out the stop sign. Tape a craft stick to the bottom to make a handle. Raise it when you hear the st consonant blend in the story.

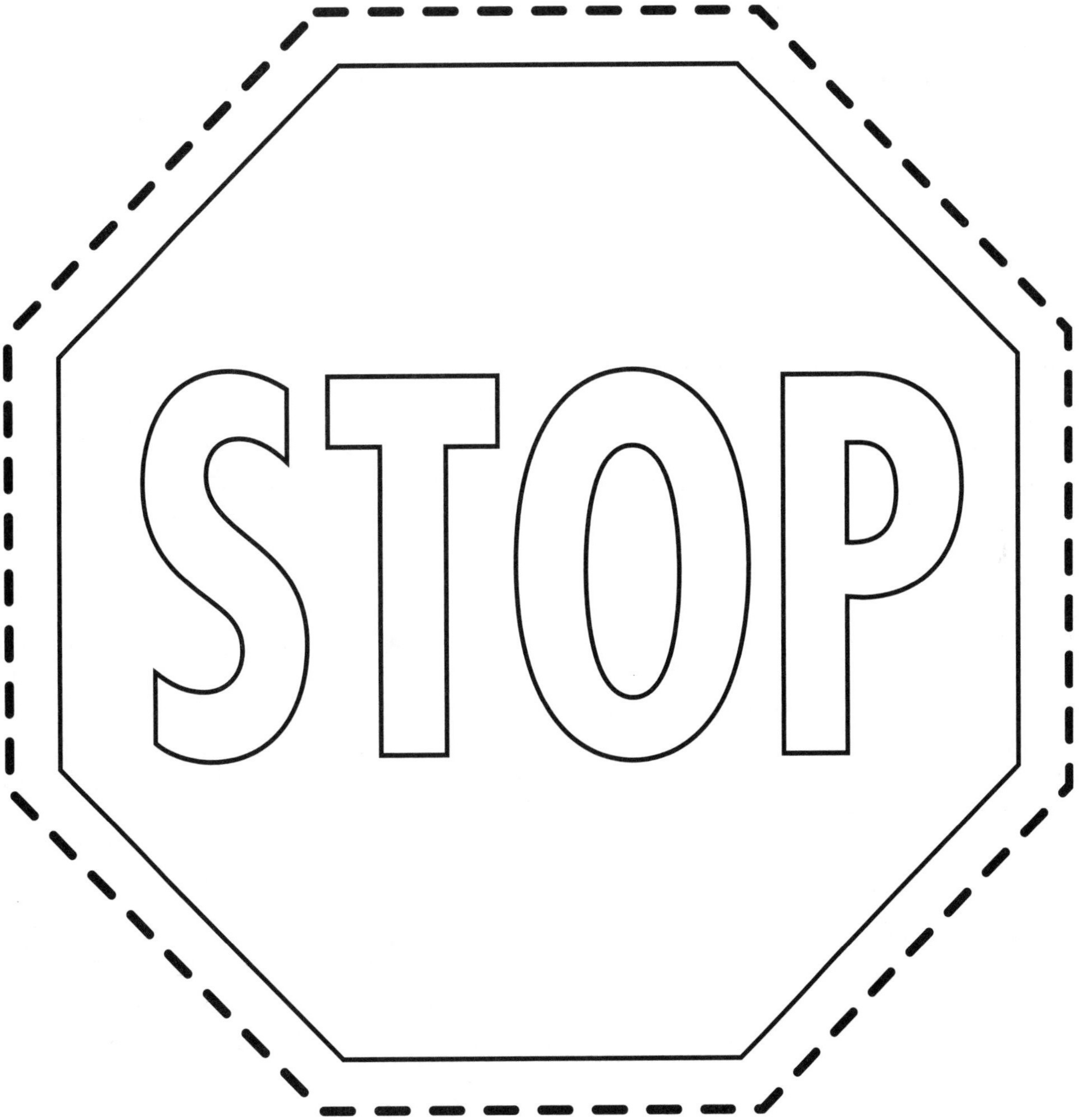

Phonics Activities
for *Livingstone Mouse*

re-reading Activity: On the board, write the following consonant digraphs: *sh, ch, th, wh, ph,* and *ng.* Explain to students that a consonant digraph is made of two consonants that stand side by side in a word but make only one sound. Review the sound of each consonant digraph listed. Show students the cover of *Livingstone Mouse.* Explain that in this story, Livingstone searches for China. Tell students that they are going to play a searching game as well. Circle *sh, th,* and *ch* on the board. Divide the class into three groups and assign a consonant digraph to each group. Provide copies of the book and tell groups to search for and write down words that contain their assigned consonant digraphs. Remind students that consonant digraphs can be found at the beginnings, middles, and ends of words. When students are finished, bring them back together and use chart paper to create three separate lists of words. Students should find the following words: *China, much, cheese, chattered, they, there, this, that, thing, then, mouthful, breathe, think, bother, thought, the, shyly, shaft, shuddering, shape,* and *trash.* Display the lists and challenge students to add relevant words they read or hear throughout the day.

uring-reading Activity: Make copies of the So Many Syllables reproducible (page 121). Have pairs cut out the syllable cards. Read these words one syllable at a time: *investigating, shuddering, cockroaches, somersaults, Livingstone, complaining, argumentative.* As you say each syllable, tell students to listen carefully and then find the card that matches. As you say the next syllables, have students line up the cards to make the word. When you have said all of the words, walk around the room to assess students' work. Since this activity will be challenging, model it before students receive the worksheets, or direct this activity at a center with small groups.

ost-reading Activity: Review the st consonant cluster with students. Have students work in pairs to search the book for words that contain the st consonant cluster. Have students write these words on the backs of their stop signs from the phonemic awareness, post-reading activity (page 118). Students should find the following words: *biggest, Livingstone, nest, must, nasty, musty, steep, stinging, post, still, stay, stop, majestically, fantastic, sting, still, just, investigating,* and *greatest.* When students finish, review the words found and make sure they have written all of the words on their stop signs. Ask students if they can think of other words to put on their stop signs. Write suggestions on the board so that students can copy them correctly. For further practice, read a list of selected words and have students hold up their stop signs every time they hear the /st/ sound.

So Many Syllables
phonics reproducible for
Livingstone Mouse

Name_____   Date _____

Cut out the syllable cards. As your teacher says a list of words, listen for the sounds that match the syllables. Use the syllable cards to make the words you hear.

in	shud	tig	ta	er
plain	roach	ves	ing	gu
saults	men	ing	com	ing
tive	at	es	der	ar
cock	Liv	ing	som	stone

Vocabulary Activities
for *Livingstone Mouse*

Pre-reading Activity: Write the following words on a piece of chart paper: *explorer, exactly, majestically, fantastic, liquid, entrance, wearily, China, china, incredible.* Leave enough room for definitions. Read each word to students and ask them if they know its definition. If students have trouble, read the following additional sentences to them to see if they can figure out the meanings from context clues: "The tired *explorer* finally found a new river. The boy knew *exactly* how much money was left. The king sat *majestically* on his black horse. The audience applauded wildly after the *fantastic* show. The ice cube melted and turned into *liquid*. The *entrance* to the cave was covered by branches. *Wearily*, the jogger finished the race in last place. The *china* teacup broke in two when it fell off the table. The *incredible* magician vanished." With your guidance, have students define each word. Write definitions next to the words on the chart.

During-reading Activity: Make copies of the Vocabulary Puzzle reproducible (page 123) for students to help them practice print awareness. Review the vocabulary words and definitions from the pre-reading activity. Tell students to listen for these words as you read the story. After reading ask if they remember hearing any words from the list. Do they remember where or when each word was used? Depending on their levels, have students either work in pairs or individually to complete the reproducible. Explain to students that each word in the gray box at the top of the page fits into a sentence at the bottom of the page. Each word must fit in its clue box exactly to make the sentence correct. Show students how to fit a word into a word box. Explain that in the first sentence, the word *explorer* fits into the box because it is the only word in the gray box that has two "regular" spaces, one space that extends down, one space that extends up, and four more "regular" spaces.

Post-reading Activity: Have students sit in a group in front of you. Display the vocabulary chart from the pre-reading activity. Review the words with students. Let students take turns choosing words and using them in sentences. Continue until all of the words have been used. Send students back to their seats. Distribute drawing paper. Explain to students that they are going to write sentences and illustrate them. Have each student pick one word from the list, write the sentence with the word at the bottom of the paper, then draw a picture to match the sentence. When students finish, have them read their sentences and show their pictures to the class.

Vocabulary Puzzle

vocabulary reproducible for
Livingstone Mouse

Name_____ Date _____

Choose a word from the word bank to write in the box in each sentence. Be careful! Each word has to fit exactly in each box. The first one has been done for you.

china   entrance   exactly

explorer   incredible   wearily

majestically   fantastic   liquid

1. Columbus was an `explorer` who sailed across the ocean to find India.

2. My mom drinks tea from a ☐ cup.

3. I could not believe my eyes when the bluebird turned pink! It was ☐ !

4. The bear pokes his head out of the ☐ of his cave.

5. My snow cone melted (turned into ☐) and dripped all over me.

6. The circus was the best, most ☐ show I ever saw!

7. The queen rode ☐ down the street wearing a crown and a robe made of jewels.

8. The puppy walked home ☐ after his long swim.

9. Tim knew ☐ how much money he had in his bank.

Fluency Activities
for *Livingstone Mouse*

Pre-reading Activity: Make copies of The Little Mouse reproducible (page 125) for students. Read the poem to students as they read it silently. Exaggerate the amount of time you pause at commas and stop at periods. Ask students if there are any words they do not understand, and review any they point out. Have students read the poem with you. Divide students into nine groups and assign each group a stanza. Give students time to practice their parts. When students are ready, have each group line up according to their stanza and read the poem. Tell students that you are looking for each group to read with the same rhythm. Practice a few times and then ask a volunteer to read the entire poem to the class.

During-reading Activity: Tell students that they are going to read *Livingstone Mouse* like a play, with students reading the parts of different characters. (You may need to repeat this activity depending on the number of students in your class.) Assign students the following parts before you read the story so they can listen for their characters to speak: Livingstone Mouse, Livingstone's mother, the click beetle, the two cockroaches, the cricket, the raccoon, the two rats, the luna moth, and the bat. Tell students that you will be the narrator. Read the story aloud. Then, place multiple copies of the book at a center for students to copy their lines. Encourage them to read fluently and with feeling. When students have had sufficient time to practice, bring them together to read the story again depending on students' levels, let students share books so they know the order of their lines, or consider having them memorize their parts and perform the story as a play.

Post-reading Activity: Livingstone Mouse is an explorer. Ask students where they would explore if they could go anywhere in the world. Tell students that you would like to write a class poem about places they would like to go. Begin by having a volunteer say a place she would like to visit. Following the example below, write her name and place as the first and last words of the first line, respectively. Challenge her to come up with the next line of the poem and help her find a word that rhymes with the place she wants to go. (Nonsense words are fine for this activity.) Continue calling on students until the poem is complete. Copy the finished poem onto a piece of poster board and have students decorate it with appropriate pictures. Let students read the poem often to build fluency and rhythm.

Cara wants to go to France,
Where, she hears, they have beautiful plants.

Juan is going to Disneyland,
He already has his vacation planned.

Shandra wants to visit New York,
Where she will dine with a knife and fork.

Name _____   Date _____

Read the poem aloud. Pause at commas and stop at periods. Practice until you can read the poem easily.

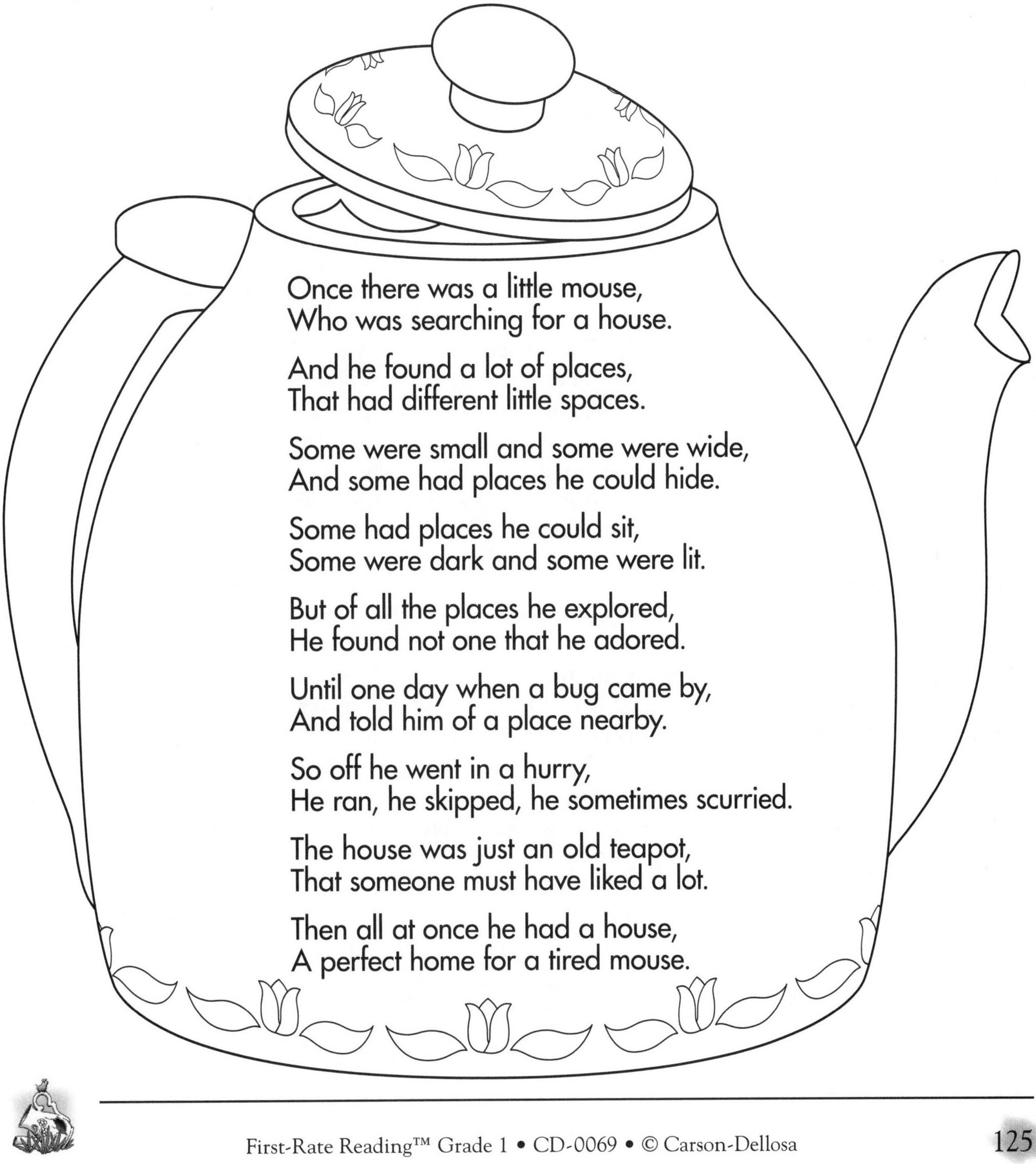

Once there was a little mouse,
Who was searching for a house.

And he found a lot of places,
That had different little spaces.

Some were small and some were wide,
And some had places he could hide.

Some had places he could sit,
Some were dark and some were lit.

But of all the places he explored,
He found not one that he adored.

Until one day when a bug came by,
And told him of a place nearby.

So off he went in a hurry,
He ran, he skipped, he sometimes scurried.

The house was just an old teapot,
That someone must have liked a lot.

Then all at once he had a house,
A perfect home for a tired mouse.

Comprehension Activities
for *Livingstone Mouse*

Pre-reading Activity: Tell students that Livingstone Mouse is an explorer who is looking for a home in China. Define the word *explorer*. Tell students that they are going to go outside to explore school grounds to find perfect houses for mice. First, explain that they should choose places that are warm and provide shelter from the weather and other animals. Have students research "mouse houses," then let each student draw two pictures. The first picture should show where and what students think would make the perfect place for a mouse to live, and the second picture should show what the inside of the house would look like. Explain that the inside of the house must have things a mouse might be able to find outside that would keep him warm and cozy such as leaves, twigs, pieces of paper, etc. Finally, let students go outside and try to find places for "mouse houses." Instruct them not to disturb any actual nests or animals. When students return to the classroom, have them show their pictures and tell whether they found similar places.

During-reading Activity: Enlarge five copies of the top half of Mouse House reproducible (page 127) and number them 1-5. Enlarge one copy of the bottom half of the reproducible and label it number 6. Tell students that Livingstone Mouse is searching for a house. As you read the story, have students listen closely to hear the places Livingstone tries to make his home. After you finish, ask students if Livingstone found China. Talk about how this is a play on words because he did end up living in china; it was just not the country. Divide the class into six groups and give a reproducible half to each. Tell each group that they must look at the number on their reproducibles to figure out which house they need to write about. Reread the house descriptions in order so students can count and know which to write about. When students finish, have them line up in order and read their sheets to retell the story of *Livingstone Mouse*.

Post-reading Activity: Divide the class into small groups and give each group a resealable plastic bag. Inform them that they are going outside to collect supplies that can be used to create houses for animals no bigger than mice. Help them brainstorm a list of animals (insects, small birds, and other small mammals, like chipmunks and moles would work.) Before going outside, remind students not to harm live plants or animals. Have them look for twigs, rocks, bark, grass, leaves, etc. Have students use the items to create shelters without using glue, since the animals don't use glue to create their habitats. (They can pile the items in shoe boxes if you have them available to simulate the small spaces many animals seek out.) Ask students in each group to identify the creature they selected to inhabit their home and why they chose the items to create its new environment.

Name_____ Date _____

Use this with the comprehension during-reading activity. Make five copies of the top half. Number them 1-5. Make one copy of the bottom half and number it 6. Have students help you fill in the sheets as you read aloud.

This house is really a _____.

This will not make a good house for Livingstone because _____

_____

_____

_____.

This is not China, says the _____.

- -

This house is really a _____.

This will make the perfect house for Livingstone because _____

_____

_____

_____.

This is China, says _____.

 _____

More Spaghetti, I Say!
by Rita Golden Gelman

(Scholastic, 1993)

Minnie the monkey loves spaghetti so much that she is too busy eating it to play. Freddy wants to play with Minnie and is frustrated that Minnie won't play with him. Then, he tries spaghetti. This book can be used to teach rhymes, verbs, plural endings, vowel digraphs, and consonant clusters.

Related books: *Cloudy with a Chance of Meatballs* by Judi Barrett (Aladdin, 1982); *Daddy Makes the Best Spaghetti* by Anna Grossnickle Hines (Clarion Books, 1999); *Strega Nona* by Tomie dePaola (Little Simon, 1997)

Phonemic Awareness Activities
for *More Spaghetti, I Say!*

Pre-reading Activity: Draw students' attention to the cover of the book and read the title aloud. Point to the word *say* and explain that ay vowel team makes a long /a/ sound. Tell students that there are two other ay words in the book (*play* and *away*). Challenge students to change the first letter(s) in *say*, *play*, and *away* to make new words.

During-reading Activity: Tell students that they will hear open syllable words in this book. Explain that an open syllable is a syllable that begins with a consonant and ends with a vowel, such as *go* and *he* or ti in *spaghetti*. Ask students to identify the letters in each of those words. As you read the book, have students fold their hands together. Every time they hear an open syllable word, have them open their hands. Students should open their hands after hearing the words *spaghetti*, *see*, *no*, *we*, *me*, and *so*, among others.

Post-reading Activity: Tell students that this book is fun to read because of the rhyming words. Use the Rhyme Match reproducible (page 129) to practice matching rhyming words. Have students cut out the pictures and place them faceup on their desks. Read a word from the following list and ask each student to hold up a picture of a rhyming word: *please*, *Freddy*, *jam*, *you*, *do*, *hide*, *air*, *and*, *head*. To extend the activity, draw pictures of objects that rhyme with story words on index cards, and repeat with the card set.

Rhyme Match

phonemic awareness reproducible for
More Spaghetti, I Say!

Name_____ Date _____

Cut out the pictures and place them faceup in front of you. As your teacher reads each word aloud, hold up a picture that rhymes with the word you hear.

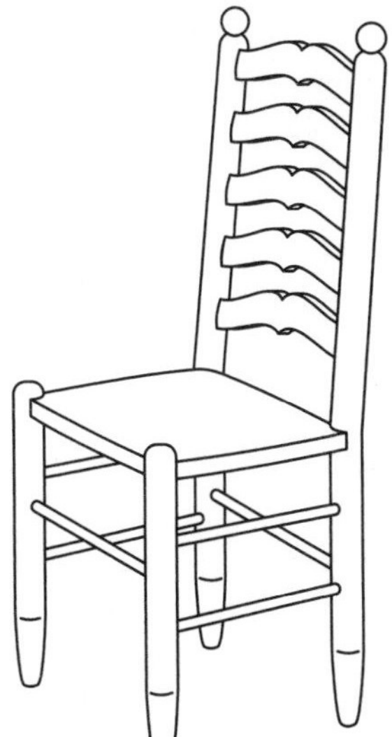

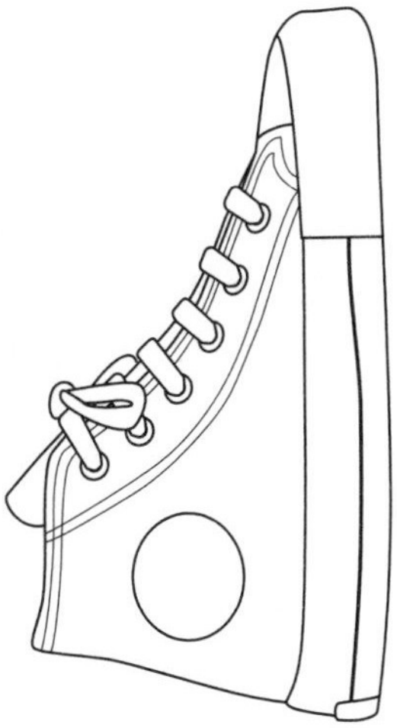

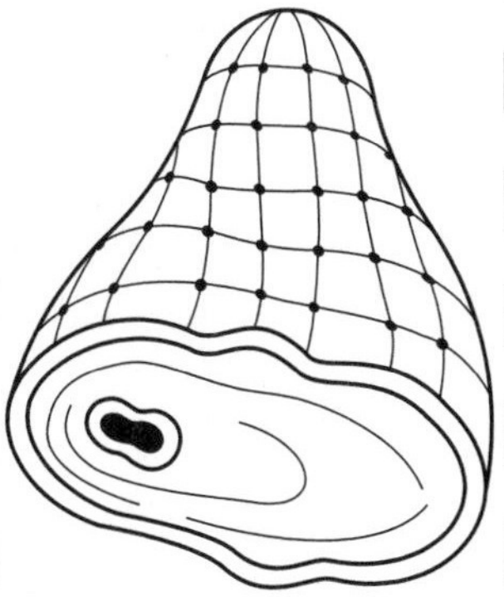

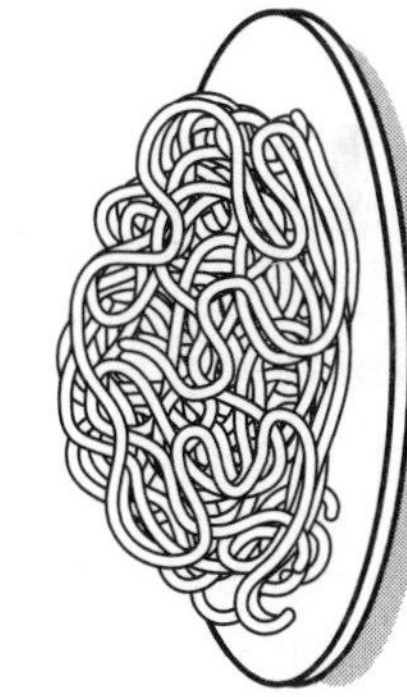

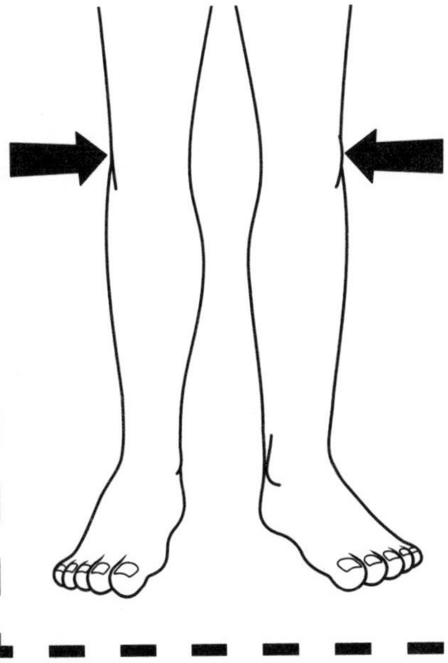

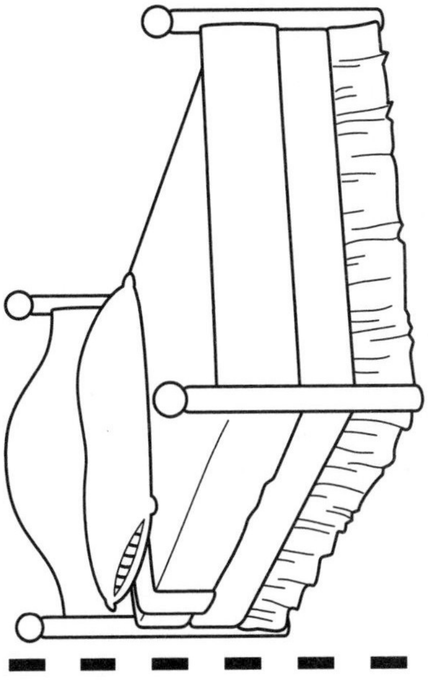

Phonics Activities
for *More Spaghetti, I Say!*

**P**re-reading Activity: Write the word *more* from the title on the board. Explain that even though there is a silent e at the end of the word, the o doesn't make the long /o/ sound because of the "bossy r." The o is r-controlled which gives it a different sound. Have students brainstorm a list of words in the ore word family such as *adore, bore, core, explore, ignore, ore, pore, sore, snore, store, tore,* and *wore.* Post the words on a bulletin board titled "More More Ore!"

During-reading Activity: Have students give examples of words with other r-controlled vowels. For example, students may suggest *barn, corn, dirt, fur,* etc. Assign students to five groups and assign one r-controlled vowel to each group. Read the book aloud, then let students reread the book in groups. As they read, have students write down words that contain their assigned r-controlled vowels. Review words that students find such as *mustard, marshmallow, more, for, floor, picture,* and *your.* Then, assign additional reading for the same purpose or have students brainstorm other words with r-controlled vowels. Finally, write each word on an index card. Place the cards in a center and give students time to sort them into piles.

Post-reading Activity: Write the sp and sl consonant blends on the board or a piece of chart paper. Explain to students that a consonant blend is made of two consonants that appear together in a word and that each letter still has its own sound, even though the sounds are blended together. Model for students how to say the sp and sl blends. Divide the class into pairs or groups and challenge them to create lists of words with consonant clusters from *More Spaghetti, I Say!* Bring students back together and create a class chart of the words. If students list words that have consonant digraphs, such as *chair, that, throw, marshmallow, should, than, please, hang,* and *enough,* explain that they are different because the two consonants in each word stand for only one sound. Then, distribute the Consonant Blends reproducible (page 131) to students. Have students cut out the consonant blends and single letters. Ask students to put the single letters together with the consonant blends to form the words on the chart. Challenge them to use the consonant blends and single letters to create other words that are not in the book. Add correctly formed words to the chart.

Name_____ Date _____

Cut out the consonant blends and single letters. Put the consonant blends together with the single letters to make words.

fl	tr	Fr	sp	pl	st
sk	sl	gr	e	e	o
o	i	u	a	d	d
r	y	n	g	h	c
k	s	s	p	t	t

Vocabulary Activities
for *More Spaghetti, I Say!*

Pre-reading Activity: On the board or a piece of chart paper, write the words *spaghetti, pancakes, ice cream, pickles, cookies, bananas, mustard, ham, jam,* and *marshmallow stuff.* Read the words to the class. Ask students how all of the words are alike (food words). Ask students what they usually eat with spaghetti. Explain to students that Minnie, a monkey in the story, loves spaghetti so much that she will eat it with almost anything. Have each student write each food word on an index card, then draw a picture of it and cut it out. Give each student a copy of the Big Bowl of Spaghetti reproducible (page 133). Ask students to predict which of these foods Minnie will eat with her spaghetti. On separate sheets of paper, have them draw the foods they think Minnie will eat, cut them out, and glue them on top of the spaghetti. Display the pictures on a bulletin board titled "Spaghetti with the Works." Check predictions after reading the story. Discuss whether students would try any of these foods with spaghetti.

During-reading Activity: Cut off the student directions and enlarge the spaghetti pattern from the Big Bowl of Spaghetti reproducible (page 133), and attach it to a bulletin board, or draw a large bowl of spaghetti on the board. Write the following words on it: *run, ride, jump, slide, hide, skate, ski, play, stand, hang, eat, look, throw, say,* and *sit.* Tell students that they will hear each of these words in the story. Tell them to listen for these words as you read the story and to make slurping noises (like slurping spaghetti) when they hear an action word from the list. (Students will love making this noise!) Practice with nonaction and action words to ensure understanding prior to beginning. Read slowly and pause slightly to allow students time to make slurping noises.

Post-reading Activity: Use the bulletin board from the during reading activity. Ask each student to choose an action word from the list to act out but have her act it out involving spaghetti. Students can pretend to stand on spaghetti, run over it, ride on it, jump in it, etc. Have other students guess the actions. If a student guesses correctly, ask him to spell the word. If he spells it correctly, let him act out another word. Continue until all words are used or each student has had a chance to act out a word. When finished, hand out drawing paper and have students draw themselves performing their funny spaghetti actions. (Consider providing cooked, cooled spaghetti for students to glue to their drawings.) Post the drawings around the bulletin board.

Name_____ Date _____

Listen to and read the food words your teacher writes. On a separate sheet of paper, draw pictures of foods you think Minnie will eat with her spaghetti. Cut out your pictures and glue them on top of the spaghetti picture.

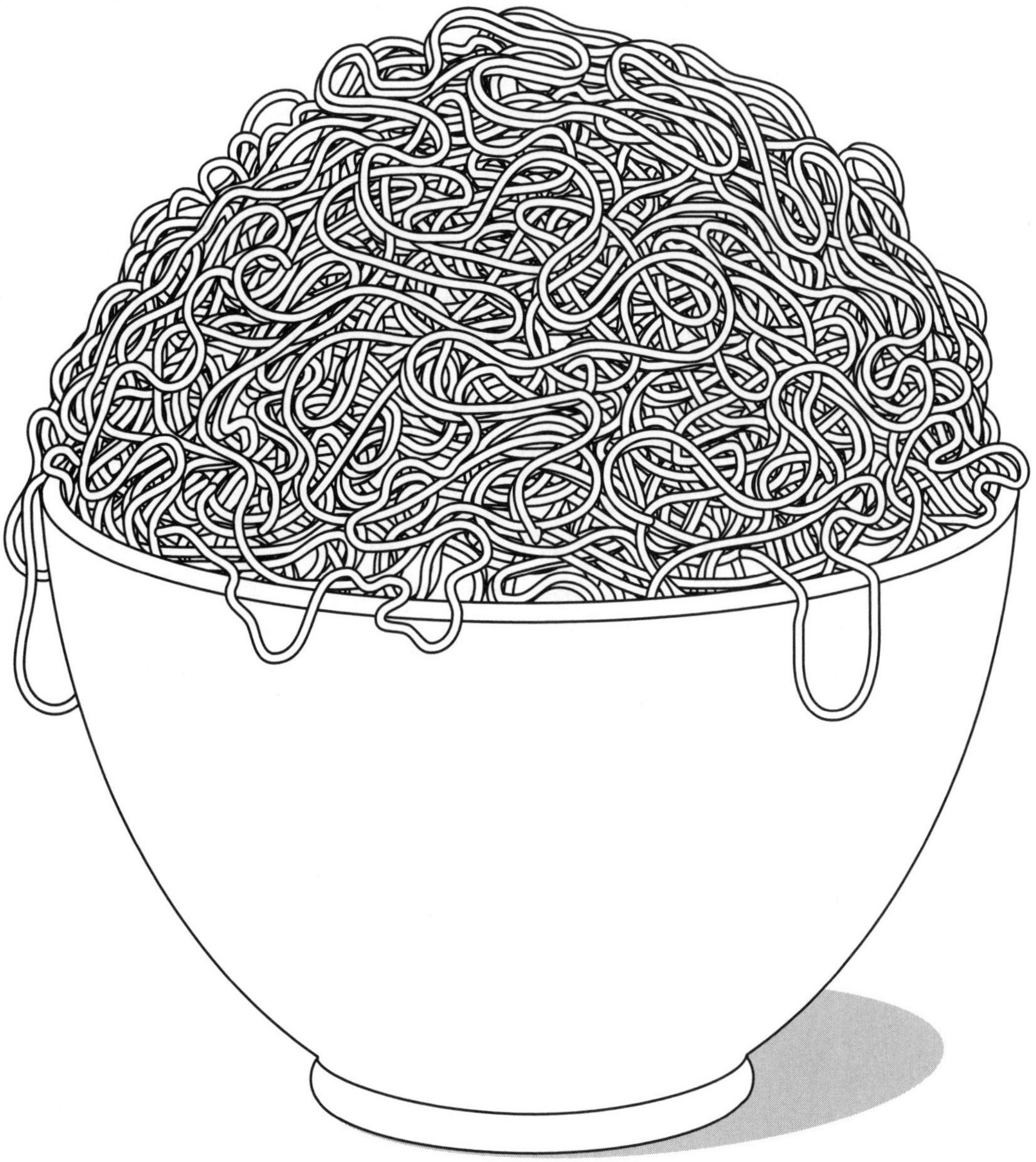

Fluency Activities
for *More Spaghetti, I Say!*

Pre-reading Activity: Explain to students that reading a rhyming book is fun because it has a rhythm. When students read the book they should practice keeping that rhythm. In this book, not only did the author use rhyme, but she also made certain words larger and put some words in bold type. When an author makes certain words larger or bold, it is to tell the reader to emphasize the words. Show students these words in the book. Tell students that they will practice reading with rhythm and emphasizing words in bold type and larger print before they read this book. Hand out copies of the Larger, Bolder, and with a Beat reproducible (page 135). Point out the words in larger print and in bold type. Model how the poem should be read. Pair students and have them practice reading the poem. After students have had time to practice, bring them back together and ask volunteers to read orally. Finally, read the poem chorally as a class. Remind students to emphasize the correct words.

During-reading Activity: Read *More Spaghetti I Say!* emphasizing words in bold type and larger print. Model the rhythm of the story. After you finish, point out the quotation marks. Explain that *quotation marks* highlight the exact words of characters in a story. Also, explain that this book has no narrator, only exact quotes from each character. Pair students and assign the parts of Minnie and Freddy to each pair. Have students practice reading their parts with each other. Challenge pairs to switch roles and try again. Then, bring students back together and ask for volunteers to read the parts of Minnie and Freddy. Remind students to read with rhythm and to emphasize words in bold type and larger print.

Post-reading Activity: Reread the poem on the Larger, Bolder, and with a Beat reproducible (page 135). Have each student make a list of favorite foods. Challenge him to write a poem about his favorite foods. If a student needs help finding rhyming words to match what he has written, have him write the words on the board and let volunteers suggest rhyming words. Tell students that they do not have to rhyme the food words; instead they can rhyme other words. For example, a student poem might read:

I like to eat candy in my **house**.
I like to eat popcorn next to my **mouse**.

Make sure that students write the rhyming words larger, in all uppercase letters, or in bolder print, for emphasis. Have students practice reading their poems with rhythm. Then, let each student read his poem aloud. For more practice, let students exchange poems to read aloud.

Name _____ Date _____

Practice reading this poem. Be sure to exaggerate the words in bold type and larger print. Remember that poems are read with rhythm. When you finish practicing, draw a picture of yourself eating spaghetti.

I **love** spaghetti
I love it a **bunch**
I eat it **all** day
And **always** for lunch!

I eat it with **meatballs**
I **top** it with cheese
I dip in my **bread**
Give me more of it, **please!**

I eat **bowls** of spaghetti
I eat every **bite**
What did you say?
No spaghetti tonight?

Comprehension Activities
for *More Spaghetti, I Say!*

Pre-reading Activity: Show the cover of the book to students. Read the title to them. Ask them what they think this story will be about. Cover the text and show students the illustrations in the book. (Do not show them the last five pages.) Draw their attention to the expressions on each character's face. Tell them that the girl monkey is Minnie and the boy monkey is Freddy. Ask them to predict what might happen in the story. Are both Minnie and Freddy happy? List all of their responses on the board or a piece of chart paper under the heading *Problems*. Ask students what they think the solutions might be. List all of their responses under the heading *Solutions*. Read the story aloud to determine if their predictions are correct.

During-reading Activity: Read *More Spaghetti, I Say!* aloud. Discuss with students the problem that Freddy has and why he is so unhappy. Discuss what happens to Minnie in the story and what happens to Freddy at the end of the story. Distribute copies of the About More Spaghetti reproducible (page 137) to students, as well as enlarged copies of the bowl of spaghetti from the Big Bowl of Spaghetti (page 133). Have them write summaries of the story on the bowls of spaghetti. (For students who have trouble getting started, give the following sentence starters: *Minnie loves _____. Freddy is unhappy because_____. Minnie gets _____. Freddy takes the spaghetti _____. Freddy tastes _____. Freddy loves _____. Now Minnie is _____.*) After students finish their summaries, have them cut out the monkeys from the reproducibles and the bowls of spaghetti. Let them staple the bowls to the monkeys' hands so that it appears as if the monkeys are holding them. Hang monkeys by their tails on strings attached to a wall or bulletin board. Add the title "Monkeys' Tales."

Post-reading Activity: Discuss how Minnie was too busy eating spaghetti to play with Freddy. Ask students to think about their favorite foods. Have each student write about what food he loves to eat and what activity it would keep him from doing. Have students write their stories and draw pictures of themselves eating their favorite foods. Then, have students read their stories aloud to the class.

Name_____ Date _____

Cut out the monkey. Write a summary of *More Spaghetti, I Say!* on the bowl of spaghetti and staple it to the monkey's hands.

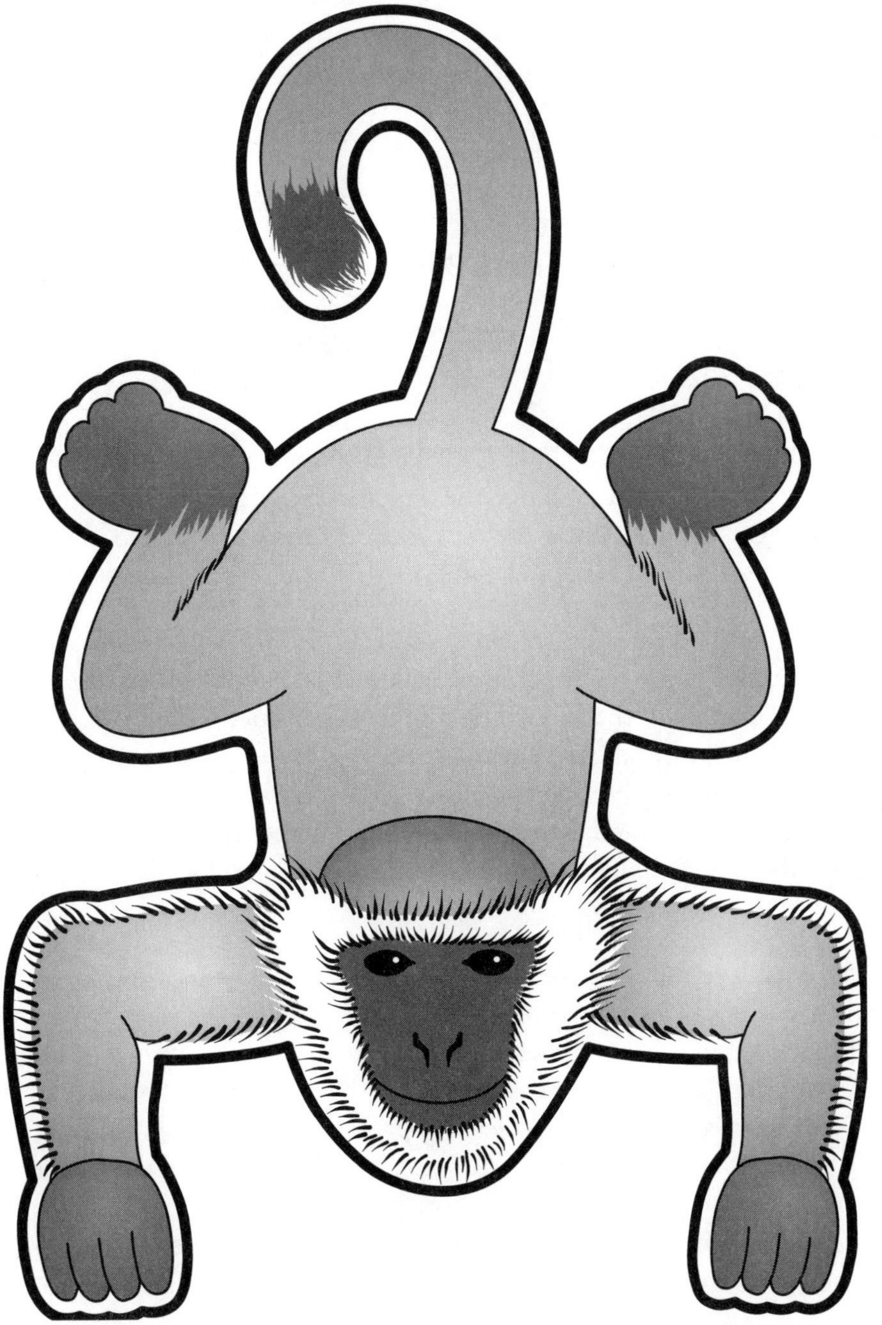

(Greenwillow Books, 1981)

On Market Street is a great beginning book because of the A to Z format and superb illustrations. The child in this story strolls down Market Street to buy gifts for a friend. *On Market Street* can be used to teach initial sounds, classification, rhyming, and creative thinking.

Related books: *Alligators All Around* by Maurice Sendak (HarperCollins, 1992); *Dr. Seuss's ABC* by Dr. Seuss (Random House, 1996); *The Z Was Zapped: A Play in 26 Acts* by Chris Van Allsburg (Houghton Mifflin, 1987)

Phonemic Awareness Activities
for *On Market Street*

Pre-reading Activity: Tell students that this book is about the alphabet. In this book, a young child will shop and buy an item that begins with each letter of the alphabet. Practice the alphabet by singing the alphabet song. Change the ending of the song by singing, "Now I know my ABC's, next time won't you shop with me?" As you sing the song, let students pretend to load shopping carts.

During-reading Activity: As you read each page to students, have them say the sound that letter makes. When you finish, go back to the beginning and have students look at each picture and say the letter, the sound the letter makes, and the item the child bought. The only pages where the letters do not have the short or common sounds are i (long sound), o (/or/ sound), and s (/sh/ sound). When you get to those pages, remind students that vowels sometimes say their names (long sound), and some letters have different sounds when they are combined with other letters.

Post-reading Activity: Use the Alphabet Picture Cards (pages 139-140) to play a shopping game with students. Use a large piece of cardboard to create a storefront. Cut out a large window so that students can stand behind it and look out. Have students color and cut out the picture cards on the reproducibles. Collect one picture card from each student to put in a container "inside" the store. Have students take turns standing behind the store window and selecting cards from the container. Each student must say the name of the picture, its initial sound, and as many words as she can think of that begin with that sound. For letters i, o, and s, let students use short vowel sounds or the usual consonant sound if necessary. Students may stay behind the window until they run out of words. Continue in this manner until each student has had a turn. Have students put the rest of their picture cards in envelopes to play with at a later time.

Alphabet Picture Cards
phonemic awareness reproducible for
On Market Street

Name_____ Date _____

Color and cut out the picture cards. Your teacher will show you how to use them to play a game.

Phonics Activities

for *On Market Street*

Pre-reading Activity: Tell students that in this story a child goes on a shopping spree. Assign a letter of the alphabet to each student. (Try not to assign the letters x, y and z because it is difficult for students to name things that begin with those letters. Create these three signs yourself to model the activity for students.) Hand out the Signs, Signs, Everywhere Signs reproducible (page 141) to students. Tell them that they are going to create store signs with their letters. Have each student write her letter on the sign and decorate the sign by drawing things that begin with her letter that can be found in the store. When students are finished, have them present their store signs and share things that can be purchased in the stores. Create a bulletin board by drawing storefronts on paper and attaching student signs to the stores. Title the board "Shop with Us on A to Z Street."

During-reading Activity: Prior to this activity, fill a container with alphabet-shaped cereal. Read the book aloud, and let students study the illustrations. Next, have each student choose a letter from the container and think of a present for a friend that begins with that letter. Have him draw a picture of the present and write the word underneath it. Have students present their work to the class when they are finished. They should read their words, show their pictures, and say why they would buy these items for their friends.

Post-reading Activity: Play an alphabet game with students. Have students sit in a circle. Start the game by saying, "I am going on a shopping trip, and I am going to buy apricots (or any other word that starts with a, including a silly word, such as 'an alligator')." Let the student next to you continue the game by saying, "I am going on a shopping trip, and I am going to buy apricots and bookmarks (or any other word that starts with b)." Continue the game by letting each student repeat her classmates' purchases and then add her own. The last student will have to repeat purchases for the entire alphabet. Consider playing again starting with the last student and moving in the opposite direction.

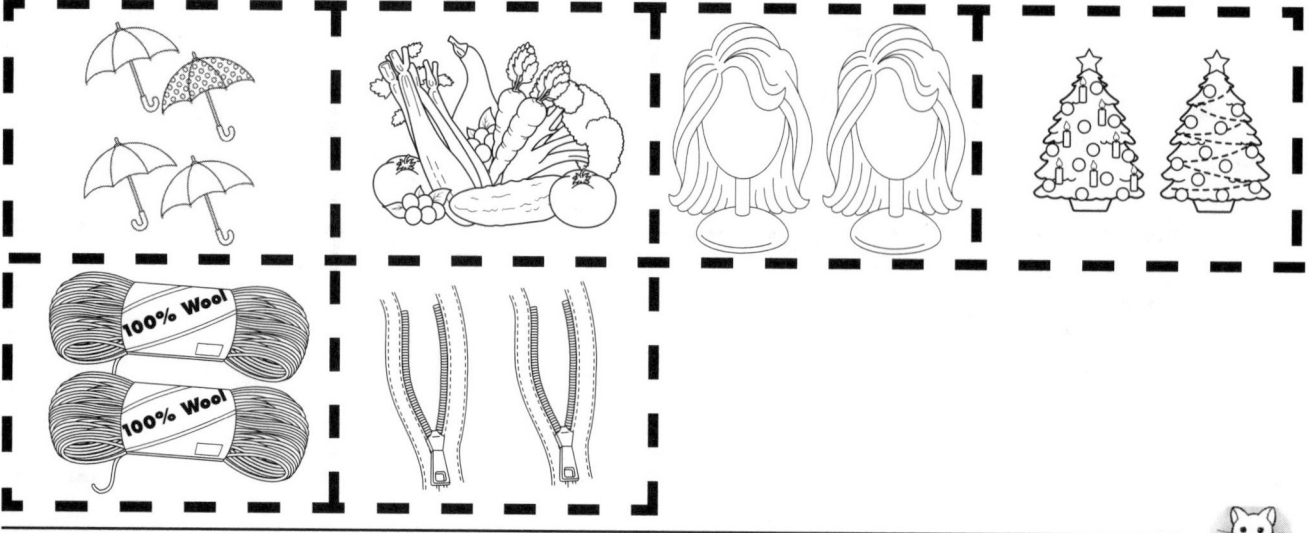

Name_____ Date _____

Write your uppercase letter on the sign. Draw objects on the sign with things you could sell in your store. You can only sell things in your store that begin with your letter.

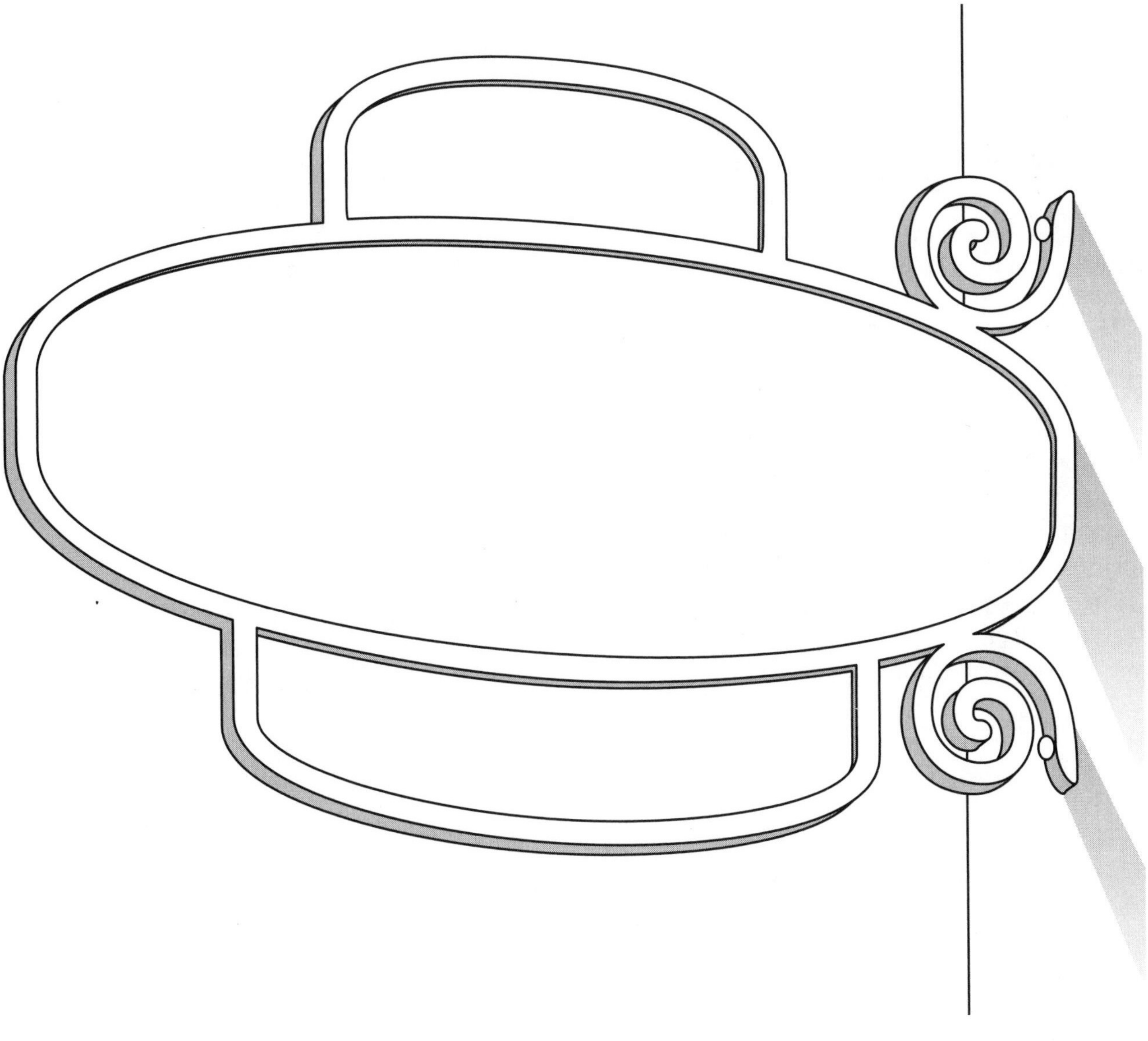

Vocabulary Activities
for *On Market Street*

Pre-reading Activity: Write the following words on the board or a piece of chart paper: *merchants, wonders, strolled, length, bought, darkness, coins, brought, spend, spent, presents*. Explain to students that some of the words in this book might be new to them. Ask if they recognize the listed words or know any of the definitions. After discussion, read the first and next-to-last pages of *On Market Street* and ask students if hearing the words in sentences helped them know what the words might mean. Let students offer definitions for words. Then, define unknown words for them. Challenge them to use any of the words in a sentence. If a sentence is correct, write it on the board and underline the vocabulary word. Continue until each word has been used in a sentence.

During-reading Activity: Show students the cover of the book. Tell them that you are going to read a story about a child who goes on a shopping spree. Tell students to think about all of the items this child buys and decide if they would buy them, too. Read the story to the class, then reread it. Ask students what the author meant when he wrote, "So much to catch my eye!" Ask each student what "catches his eye" when he goes shopping. Hand out copies of the Shopping Spree reproducible (page 143). Have students complete them individually. Share shopping lists when students are finished and use the new vocabulary students listed in other vocabulary activities.

Post-reading Activity: Draw students' attention to the illustrations in the book. Discuss how creative the illustrator was when she created the characters. Ask students which pictures they like best and why. Assign a letter of the alphabet to each student. (If you do not have 26 students, have students who finish first create second pictures, or create some of your own.) Challenge each student to think of an item that starts with her letter and draw a character made entirely of that item. Have students color their pictures and write the names of the items used to create the characters. Create a bulletin board of their finished characters. Cut out a large letter to put above each drawing and write the word under the drawing. Title the display "A Parade of Characters from A to Z." Use the items students chose as weekly vocabulary words.

Shopping Spree

vocabulary reproducible for
On Market Street

Name_____ Date _____

If you went on a shopping spree, what would you buy? What would "catch your eye" in each store? When you are in each type of store, what do you see that you always want? Fill in the blanks.

In the grocery store, _____ would catch my eye.

In the toy store, _____ would catch my eye.

In the clothing store, _____ would catch my eye.

In the hobby store, _____ would catch my eye.

In the stationery store, _____ would catch my eye.

In the book store, _____ would catch my eye.

In the candy shop, _____ would catch my eye.

In the bakery, _____ would catch my eye.

In the pet store, _____ would catch my eye.

In the ice cream shop, _____ would catch my eye.

In the video store, _____ would catch my eye.

In the flower shop, _____ would catch my eye.

In the athletic store, _____ would catch my eye.

Fluency Activities
for *On Market Street*

Pre-reading Activity: Tell students that in this story a young child goes to a market to buy presents for a friend. Distribute the To Market, To Market reproducible (page 145) and have students practice the nursery rhyme "To Market, To Market" to help them with fluency. Read the poem once to students. Before they begin to practice the poem, remind them to pause at commas and stop at periods. After students have practiced individually, assign the first stanza to half of the class and the second stanza to the other half. Tell students to read the third stanza together. Afterwards, challenge students to change the animal in the second line of each stanza and the last syllable in the last line to rhyme with the new arrival. For example:

To market, to market
To buy a fat hen.
Home again, home again,
Jiggety-jen.
or
To market, to market
To buy a fat cow.
Home again, home again,
Jiggety-jow.

During-reading Activity: Tell students that parts of *On Market Street* rhyme and others don't. Have them listen to see if they can find the rhyming parts as you read the story. Reread the first and last pages, and ask why these parts are different. (They rhyme.) Divide the class into two groups. Have one group find the rhyming words on the first page and the other groups find the rhyming words on the last two pages. Compare and contrast the rhyming words and note how the rhymes in poems show how to put emphasis on certain words. Students should find *doors/stores, eye/buy, more/sore,* and *spend/friend.* Read the first and last two pages together chorally. Practice until students read with rhythm and fluency.

Post-reading Activity: Ask students what presents they would like to receive. Ask if they have ever made a wish list. Tell each student that she is going to make a special wish list—it is going to have 26 items on it. Ask if they can guess why they will have 26 items. Tell each student she must have a present for each letter of the alphabet. Have students create rough drafts of the lists first so that you can check spelling and number of items. Then, have students write their lists on oversized sheets of paper. Ask each student to read her list to a partner as fluently as she can, pausing as if there were a comma after each item. Roll up these lists and tie them with ribbons to send home, or display them on a wall or bulletin board with the title "Plenty of Presents."

First-Rate Reading™ Grade 1 • CD-0069 • © Carson-Dellosa

Name_____ Date _____

Read the nursery rhyme below. Make sure you pause at commas and stop at periods. Remember to read at a steady pace, just like you talk. If you have time, write a new verse on the lines provided, and practice reading it as well. Draw a picture of your verse.

To Market, To Market

To market, to market,
To buy a fat pig.
Home again, home again,
Jiggety-jig.

To market, to market,
To buy a fat hog.
Home again, home again,
Jiggety-jog.

To market, to market,
To buy a plum bun.
Home again, home again,
Market is done.

_____

_____

_____

_____

_____

Comprehension Activities
for *On Market Street*

Pre-reading Activity: Show the cover of the book to students and read the title. Ask students if they know the definition of *market*. Ask them what they see on the cover. Why do they think this child has these items? Did he buy them? Why? Ask students what the boy is holding closest to him (apples). Ask, "What is the first letter in the word *apple* (a)?" Next to the apples are books. Ask, "What is the first letter in the word *book* (b)?" Continue until students realize that the child buys things that start with letters of the alphabet.

During-reading Activity: Ask students who the child might be buying all of these things for. Create a list of their responses. Read the story to students, then explain that all of these things were bought as presents for a friend. Who was the friend? Show the last page of the book and ask students to identify the only thing in the picture that the child did not buy (the cat). Tell students that the cat must be a very good friend to the child! Finally, have each student write a story in which he chooses a friend for whom he would like to buy presents, and names three items from the book that his friend would like and why. Provide sentence starters, if needed. For example: I would like to buy presents for _____. I would buy _____, _____, and _____ because_____. Have students draw pictures of their friends with their presents.

Post-reading Activity: Put items on a table that students can classify into groups, such as chalk, an eraser, paper, an apple, a box of crackers or cookies, a container of milk, a hat, gloves, and eyeglasses. Have students look carefully at all of the items. Ask them to name similar items. (They may suggest things used in school, things to eat or drink, things to wear, etc.) Accept any combination of items as long as each student can give a reason for her combination. Tell students that they have just *classified* the items. Write the word *classify* on the board. Write the definition next to the word. Next, discuss the different types of items the child in the book buys. Hand out the Classification reproducible (page 147). Direct students to reread the book to classify all of the presents the child bought into the categories on the reproducible. Students may work in pairs or groups. Review all pages orally with students. Tell students that there are no wrong answers as long as they can tell you their reasons for classifying items. Accept any reasonable explanation. To extend the activity, let students create four categories of their own and sort the items again.

First-Rate Reading™ Grade 1 • CD-0069 • © Carson-Dellosa

Classification
comprehension reproducible for
On Market Street

Name_____ Date _____

Use the book *On Market Street* to classify, or put in groups, all of the presents the child bought.

Things We Wear

_____
_____
_____
_____
_____
_____
_____
_____

Things We Play With

_____
_____
_____
_____
_____
_____
_____
_____

Things We Eat

_____
_____
_____
_____
_____
_____
_____

Things We Use

_____
_____
_____
_____
_____
_____
_____

One of Each

by Mary Ann Hoberman

(Scholastic, 1998)

Oliver Tolliver is pleased with his house that has one of each item, until he invites Peggoty Small to visit. Peggoty is not impressed that Oliver has one of each item. She points out that it is not a house where friends could visit. Oliver considers what Peggoty tells him and goes on a shopping trip to help his house accommodate guests. Peggoty visits again and expresses her pleasure with the changes. Soon Oliver is visited by many new friends.

Related books: *Come Over to My House* by Theo. Le Sieg (Random House, 1973); *A House Is a House for Me* by Mary Ann Hoberman (Puffin, 1982)

Phonemic Awareness Activities
for *One of Each*

Pre-reading Activity: Before reading the story, introduce a lesson on rhyming words. Explain that some words sound the same at the end. Explain that the words *cap* and *map* are rhyming words because they both end with /ap/. Ask students to listen as you say *cap*, *map*, and *tap*. Ask if *tap* rhymes with *cap* and *map*. Then, ask students to offer other words that end with /ap/. Continue using this exercise with other words that appear in the story such as *bed*, *feet*, *me*, *call*, and *pink*. This will prepare students to recognize some of the rhyming words in the text.

During-reading Activity: After you introduce the story, explain that it is written in verse like a poem and that words will rhyme at the ends of different lines. Ask students to listen for rhyming words as you read the story. After reading each page aloud, ask students to identify the rhyming words. They might recall some of the words they worked with in the pre-reading activity. Select another rhyming pair not yet addressed such as *book* and *look*. Ask students to think of other words that end with the /ook/ sound. Repeat this exercise with the following pairs: *thing/king*, *floor/more*, and *fit/it*.

Post-reading Activity: Use the picture cards on the One of Each Card reproducible (page 149) to play a rhyming game. Decorate a shoe box to look like a house. Have students help you color and cut out one set of the picture cards. Put the cards in the house. Ask a student to take a card from the house and tell the rest of the class the name of the picture. Have students take turns offering rhyming words until they can't think of others. Then, let another student select a card. Continue the game until each student gets a chance to select a card. Let students make their own card sets for individual practice.

One of Each Card

phonemic awareness reproducible for
One of Each

Have students color and cut out the picture cards. Place them in a shoe box house. Play the game described in the post-reading phonemic-awareness activity. Have students place the remaining cards in envelopes for future work on rhyming words.

Phonics Activities
for *One of Each*

Pre-reading Activity: Point out the word *each* in the title of the book. Explain that the ea in the word *each* makes the long /e/ sound. Write the words *he*, *see*, and *peach* on index cards. Point out the single e, ee, and ea patterns in the words and explain that all have the long /e/ sound. Ask students to share other words in which they hear the long /e/ sound. Write students' words on index cards and point out that the long /e/ sound can be made with many spelling patterns. Have students work with you or in small groups to search *One of Each* to find all of the words containing one of the three letter patterns. Students should find *the*, *he*, *be*, *me*, *delight*, *idea*, *see*, *street*, *meet*, *sheet*, *feet*, *agree*, *glee*, *speech*, *each*, *teach*, *peach*, *reach*, *pleased*, *eat*, *dearie*, *dreary*, *tea*, *teacup*, and *eating*. Students may also point out *pear* (which is not a long /e/ word), *cheerful* (which is r-controlled), and *piece* (which is a long /e/ word but has a different spelling pattern). Have students say each word and then make more cards to add to the set. Collect all of the cards and then give one to each student. Ask each student to first read his word and identify the spelling pattern, then search the room for other students that have cards with words that contain the same pattern. Ask students to check to make sure they are in the correct groups and take turns reading their words to the groups. Once they have practiced the words in groups, ask students to share the words with the class and point out the spelling pattern in each word.

During-reading Activity: Explain that there are many long words in this story. Introduce the concept of syllabication as a method of decoding words. Have students look at a two-syllable story word, such as *around*, and say it as they hold their hands under their chins. Explain to them that when they say the word, their chins will drop down twice because it is a two-syllable word. Explain that a *syllable* is a word part, and that each syllable must contain a vowel. As you read the book to students, make them aware that most lines in the story end with one-syllable words but some end with two-syllable words. At the end of each line, have students say the last word with their hands under their chins to determine if it is a one- or two-syllable word. They should be able to find the following two-syllable words: *cupboard*, *pleasure*, *treasure*, *explain*, *agree*, *alone*, *about*, *admit*, *accord*, *before*. Point out the different vowels in each syllable of each two-syllable word.

Post-reading Activity: Continue the discussion concerning words with more than one syllable. Explain that when a word contains a double consonant, it is divided between the consonants. Have students work in pairs to find words in the book with double consonants. They should be able to find *cannot*, *hurried*, *arranged*, *nibbled*, *little*, *pillow*, *happy*, *happen*, *bottle*, *mirror*, *missing*, *arrived*, *better*, *accord*, *cheerfully*, *jolly*, *offer*, *carefully*, *collection*, *Peggoty* and *Tolliver*. If they suggest *passed* and *dressed*, explain that the ed is an ending that doesn't always make a new syllable. Review the four three-syllable words. Then, write each word on an index card and write the number of syllables on the back. Have students use the cards to play the game on the Syllable Sort reproducible (page 151).

Name _____ Date _____

Use two buttons for game pieces and use the syllable cards your teacher made to play Syllable Sort with a partner. Place the cards in a pile with the words faceup. Draw a card. If you can say the word correctly and identify the number of syllables, move that many spaces on the board. Take turns until someone reaches Oliver Tolliver's house to win the game.

Start

Vocabulary Activities
for *One of Each*

Pre-reading Activity: Discuss that some of the words in the book are hard but that students can use their decoding skills to figure them out. Write these words on index cards: *Oliver, Tolliver, delight, collection, certainly, carefully, bureau, treasure, enjoyment, pleasure, explain, perfectly, dreary, Peggoty, arranged, friendlier, invited, arrived, cavorted, accord, sharpened, polished.* Help students use familiar parts of the words to figure them out. Use them in sentences to help students understand their meanings. Ask students to think of synonyms for these words. Then, play a game to sharpen students' skills. Post the index cards on a bulletin board and gather the class in a semicircle around the display. Take a card from the board and hand it to the first student in the semicircle. Have him use the word in a sentence. If he is incorrect, give him clues to help him figure it out. If he is correct, allow him to choose a different word and give it to the next student in line. If there are more students than cards, start over and reuse word cards.

During-reading Activity: Use the word cards created for the pre-reading activity to initiate a lesson on vocabulary, word recognition, and print awareness. Give each student a vocabulary card and a chenille craft stick to hold as you read *One of Each*. As you read the story, ask students to listen for the vocabulary words that they are holding. When students see and hear their words, invite them to come up and match them with the words in the story. Then, write each word on the board and let each student bend her chenille craft stick around the word to frame it. Some students may need to frame their words more than once.

Post-reading Activity: Ask students to identify all of the items in Oliver Tolliver's house. Cut out the cards on the Oliver's Objects reproducible (page 153). Explain that the cards have names of things in Oliver's house. Show them to students and have them identify the words. Explain that their classroom may contain some of the same items as in Oliver's house. Tell them that they will search the classroom to see if they can identify the items that the cards name. Put double-sided tape on the back of each card and give one to each student. Have her decide the proper place in the classroom to tape her object name card. (Students may not be able to find some of the objects in the classroom such as sink and footstool. Let those students draw their objects on the board.) Have students share their placement of the cards with classmates. Make a second set of the cards and place them in a reading center. Allow each student to use them to search the room to find the same objects (or words, if you continue to display the cards), and also to write a sentence for each word in a writing journal.

Name_____ Date _____

Have students use these cards with the vocabulary post-reading activity (page 152).

window	door	carpet
floor	chair	closet
sink	cupboard	clock
bookcase	book	mirror
bottle	footstool	cup

Fluency Activities
for *One of Each*

Pre-reading Activity: Point out that in *One of Each*, students will read about a dog named Oliver Tolliver who has a house. Ask students to determine what might be in Oliver Tolliver's house by reading the title. Introduce the story by discussing that it is written in verse. Allow students to preview some of the italicized phrases about the house's contents. Choose some from the beginning and some from later in the book. Compare them and discuss how the phrases sound as the story continues. This will prepare students for the rhythm and rhyme of the story as they hear it read to them. Have students clap the rhythm as you read aloud.

During-reading Activity: The author has created a perfect construction for students to read aloud. Write the italicized lines from pages 5, 10, 18, 25, and 30 on the board or a transparency. Practice the lines aloud while coaching students to read them fluently and rhythmically. Read the book aloud and pause on these pages to indicate where students should read these lines.

Post-reading Activity: Oliver Tolliver has an unusual name. Point out that his last name rhymes with his first name. Play a name game with students to help them understand sound patterns in their own names. Start with *Peggoty*. Ask what last name they could give her that sounds like her first name. Offer words like *Sweggoty*, *Jeggoty*, and *Regotty* as examples. Give students copies of the Oliver Tolliver reproducible deproducible (page 155) to help them practice. Challenge students to give themselves new last names by thinking of the sound patterns in their first names. For example, students' new names might be Joey Doey, Amy Hamy, Sabena Mabena, Erin Sterin, etc. Have them repeat the names to hear the patterns. To celebrate reading this book, consider making name tags for students to wear during reading time. Encourage students to call each other by their new names for a day. Then, let students chorally read the book aloud, putting extra emphasis on the rhymes.

Name_____ Date _____

Oliver Tolliver has a name that rhymes. What would it sound like if they had silly rhyming last names? Practice with Peggoty Small, then make up a rhyming first and last name for each character below.

Peggoty _____

_____

_____

_____

_____

_____

Comprehension Activities
for *One of Each*

Pre-reading Activity: Inform students that the setting for *One of Each* is a house. Ask them to name some of the things that they have in their own homes like tables, chairs, or couches. Tell them that the items they suggest can be in a bedroom, kitchen, or living room. As they give you suggestions, write the names of the items on index cards and place them in a pocket chart or tape them to the board. Cut out a large house shape by cutting off the top corners of a piece of poster board or draw one on the board. Divide the house into three columns labeled *kitchen, bedroom,* and *living room*. Ask students to help you tape the index cards in the correct columns to determine what things should be in each room. Remind them that some items may be able to fit in more than one room. They will have to decide in which room to place them since, just like Oliver, they only have one of each. Explain to students that what they are doing is called *classification*. They are putting things together according to certain characteristics. Ask them to think of other ways they can classify the items. Categories could be things that have legs, things that are soft, things that are smaller than a student desk, etc.

During-reading Activity: As you read the story, ask students to consider the following questions and listen for information that will help them find the answers. Why did Oliver only have one of each item in his house at the beginning of the story? Who visits Oliver at his house and how does she feel about the visit? Why did Oliver buy one more of everything for his house? How did Oliver's life change when he filled his house with pairs of things? Was Oliver happy or sad at the end of the story? Why? After you read the story, have students work in pairs and share their answers with each other. Then, have students share their ideas with the class.

Post-reading Activity: Discuss how Oliver decided that having pairs of things was better than having one of each. Talk about the meaning of the word *pairs*. Offer students examples of different things that come in pairs, such as socks and gloves. Explain that some pairs can be things that go together but are not alike such as a cup and saucer. Play a game with students. Divide the class into two teams. Have members of each team take turns offering names for pairs of things. Some pairs to expect are eyes, ears, socks, shoes, mittens, gloves, paper and pencil, needle and thread, knife and fork, salt and pepper, and peanut butter and jelly. The game ends when a team cannot think of more pairs. Use the game to initiate a discussion about how people can be perfect pairs. Explain that what Oliver really learned was that it wasn't much fun to be alone with just one of each item for himself. It was much more fun to have friends. He found that it was easier to have friends visit after he placed pairs of things in his home. They didn't come because the things were nice, they came because he invited them and did something nice for them by sharing. (This part of the lesson is important so that students don't think having more things is a way to have more friends.) Ask students to think of what makes someone a good friend. After generating a list of qualities, have them use the Fabulous Friends reproducible (page 157) to write about the qualities of good friends. Post the finished papers on a bulletin board and title it "Perfect Pairs."

First-Rate Reading™ Grade 1 • CD-0069 • © Carson-Dellosa

Fabulous Friends

comprehension reproducible for
One of Each

Name_____ Date _____

Write what you think being a good friend means by filling in the sentence starter. Add as many qualities as you think are important. Then, color the figures to look like you and a friend of yours.

A friend is _____.

This answer key includes information for pages that have definite answers. Also included are names of all pictures students are asked to identify. Answers are not included for drawing activities, activities in which students hold up cards during reading, storytelling activities, manipulative spelling activities, and other activities where individual and group participation are oral.

Chickens Aren't the Only Ones by Ruth Heller

page 21: Assembled puzzle should spell (from top to bottom) crocodile, hummingbird, dinosaur, octopus, anteater, platypus.
page 23: Picture names are chameleon, salamander, giant clam, butterfly, fish, crocodile, ostrich, hummingbird, frog, sea horse, housefly, octopus. Students should draw lines to match chameleon/crocodile, giant clam/octopus, fish/sea horse, ostrich/hummingbird, frog/salamander, housefly/butterfly.

The Foot Book by Dr. Seuss

page 39: Picture names are bee, hood, book, knee, hook, football, leaf, peach. Hood, book, hook, and football should be sorted into the foot pile. Bee, knee, leaf, and peach should be sorted into the feet pile.

The Grouchy Ladybug by Eric Carle

page 49: Picture names are yellow jacket, stag beetle, praying mantis, sparrow, lobster, skunk, boa constrictor, hyena, gorilla, rhinoceros, elephant, whale, ladybug.
page 53: Yellow jacket is showing its stinger, stag beetle is opening its jaws, praying mantis is reaching out with its front legs, sparrow is opening its sharp beak, lobster is stretching its claws, skunk is starting to lift its tail, boa constrictor says "right after lunch," hyena is laughing eerily and showing its teeth, gorilla is beating its chest, rhinoceros is lowering its horn, elephant is raising its trunk and showing its big tusks. The whale (not on the sheet) did not answer, but the whale's tail gave the grouchy ladybug such a slap. . .
page 57: Answers will vary. 1. The grouchy ladybug was rude to the friendly ladybug. It asked if the friendly ladybug wanted to fight. 2. The grouchy ladybug used bad manners by acting like all of the other animals were in the way, even though they were there first. 3. It was not smart, because fighting isn't smart and because all of the other animals were much bigger. 4. The grouchy ladybug had asked many other animals to fight, but was afraid to go through with it. When the friendly ladybug was friendly a second time, the grouchy ladybug was hungry and tired, and maybe sorry for acting rudely. 5. The grouchy ladybug learned to be polite and not to pick fights.

The Hat by Jan Brett

page 59: Picture names are cow, hen, gander, cat, dog, pig, pony, duck.

If You Take a Mouse to School by Laura Joffe Numeroff

page 69: Picture names are paper, cookies, notebook, yo-yo, milk, books, pencil, eraser, ball, stapler, backpack, sandwich, pen, juice, crayons, cards.
page 71: Students should fill in letters to make the words mouse, school, lunchbox, snack, notebook, pencils, backpack, math, wash, lunchroom, blocks, house, books, home, tuck, shoot, stops, back.
page 73: Words should be used in this order: write, right; sum, some; won, one; four, for; see, sea; to, too, two.

Is Your Mama a Llama? by Deborah Guarino

page 79: Picture names are kangaroo, seal, swan, bat, llama, cow.
page 83: Answers will vary. 1 and 6 should be asked. 5 should be explained.
page 85: Answers will vary. Punctuation may be used in this order: . ? . ! ! ! ? . .
page 87: Picture names are kangaroo, bat, swan, seal, llama, cow, cria, joey, pup, pup, cygnet, calf. Pictures should be pasted together in the following pairs: kangaroo/joey, bat/(bat)pup, swan/cygnet, seal/(seal)pup, llama/cria, cow/calf.

Answer Key for Activity Pages

It Looked Like Spilt Milk by Charles G. Shaw

page 89: Shape names are hat, square, dog, star, boat, tree. Picture names are cat, rat, bat, bear, pear, frog, log, coat, jar, car, goat, note, bee, key. Students should match hat/cat/rat/bat; square/bear/pear; dog/frog/log; star/jar/car; boat/coat/goat/note; tree/bee/key.

The Itsy Bitsy Spider by Iza Trapani

page 101: Spiders should be matched with clothespins to make the words web, fan, slipped, sun, and stop.

Jamaica's Find by Juanita Havill

page 113: Answers may vary; words can be used in this order: stuffed, rolled, shouting, stopped, looked, watching, stayed, feeling, tossed, climbed, squeezed, dropped, looked, playing, squeezed, hugging, feeling.

page 117: Answers will vary. In the first part of the story, Jamaica was happy because she found a toy. In the middle of the story, Jamaica was sad because she knew the toy belonged to someone else. At the end of the story, Jamaica was proud because she returned the toy and made a friend.

Livingstone Mouse by Pamela Duncan Edwards

page 121: Students should make the following words: investigating, shuddering, cockroaches, somersaults, Livingstone, complaining, argumentative.

page 123: 1. explorer 2. china 3. incredible 4. entrance 5. liquid 6. fantastic 7. majestically 8. wearily 9. exactly

page 127: 1. The house is really a tool cabinet; it did not make a good house because it was too noisy; the click beetle said it was not China. 2. The house is really a sneaker; it did not make a good house because it was too smelly; the cricket said it was not China. 3. The house is really a picnic basket; it did not make a good house because it was too hot (spicy); the raccoon said it was not China. 4. The house is really a trap; it did not make a good house because it hurt; the rats said it was not China. 5. The house is really a lamppost; it did not make a good house because it was too bright; the luna moth said it was not China. 6. The house is really a china teapot; it made a perfect house because it was warm and dry and had two escape hatches; the bat said it was china.

More Spaghetti, I Say! by Rita Golden Gelman

page 129: Picture names are chair (rhymes with air), shoe (rhymes with you, do), ham (rhymes with jam), spaghetti (rhymes with Freddy), knees (rhymes with please), slide (rhymes with hide), and bed (rhymes with head).

page 131: Some story words students can make are Freddy, spaghetti, play, please, stand, chair, that, green, etc.

On Market Street by Arnold Lobel

pages 139 and 140: Picture names are apples, books, clocks, doughnuts, eggs, flowers, gloves, hats, ice cream, jewels, kites, lollipops, musical instruments, noodles, oranges, playing cards, quilts, ribbons, shoes, toys, umbrellas, vegetables, wigs, Xmas trees, yarn, zippers.

page 147: Answers may vary. Things we wear: gloves, hats, jewels, ribbons, shoes, wigs, zippers. Things we play with: kites, musical instruments, playing cards, toys. Things we eat: apples, doughnuts, eggs, ice cream, lollipops, noodles, oranges, vegetables. Things we use: books, clocks, flowers, quilts, umbrellas, Xmas trees, yarn.

One of Each by Mary Ann Hoberman

page 149: Picture names are coat, cat, bed, jar, pig, hen, mouse, stop, door, king, bug, vest, map, tag, nose, hook, stork, net, cake, stairs.

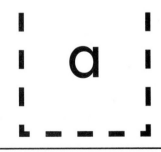

Alphabet Cards

b	c	d	e	f
g	h	i	j	k
l	m	n	o	p
q	r	s	t	u
v	w	x	y	z

First-Rate Reading™ Grade 1 • CD-0069 • © Carson-Dellosa